EXPLORE THE WORLD

CW00692463

EGYPT

Author:
Eva Ambros

*An Up-to-date travel guide
with 37 color photos
and 20 maps*

NELLES

LEGEND / IMPRINT

Dear Reader: Being up-to-date is the main goal of the Nelles series. Our correspondents help keep us abreast of the latest developments in the travel scene, while our cartographers see to it that maps are also kept completely current. However, as the travel world is constantly changing, we cannot guarantee that all the information contained in our books is always valid. Should you come across a discrepancy, please contact us at: Nelles Verlag, Schleissheimer Str. 371 b, 80935 Munich, Germany, tel. (089) 3571940, fax (089) 35719430, e-mail: Nelles.Verlag@t-online.de
Note: Distances, measurements and temperatures used in this guide are metric.
For conversion information, please see the *Guidelines* section of this book.

LEGEND

★★ ★★	Main Attraction *(on map)* *(in text)*	**Ad-Dair** *(Town)* Kalabsha *(Sight)*	Places Highlighted in Yellow Appear in Text		═══════	Motorway, expressway
★ ★	Worth Seeing *(on map)* *(in text)*	◄ ◄	Int'l Airport, Nat'l Airport		───────	Principal Highway
❽	Orientation Number in Text and on Map	**Alfabia** 1067	Mountain (altitude in meters)		───────	Main Road
▪	Public or Significant Building	\ 13 /	Distance in Kilometers		───────	Secondary Road
▪	Hotel	☀	Beach		─ ─ ─ ─	Minor road, track
○	Market	∪	Watering point, well		───────	Railway
🄳	Tourist Information	▲	Pyramid		77	Road numbering
✝ ☾	Church, Mosque	∴	Ancient site		⑤⑤⑤ ⑤⑤ ⑤	Luxury Hotel Category Moderate Hotel Category Budget Hotel Category
⛪	Monastery	✕	Mine, quarry			*(for price information see "Accomodation" in Guidelines section)*

EGYPT
© Nelles Verlag GmbH, 80935 München
All rights reserved

First Edition 2001
ISBN 3-88618-825-6 (Nelles Travel Pack)
ISBN 3-88618-824-8 (Nelles Pocket)
Printed in Slovenia

Publisher:	Günter Nelles	**Photo Editor:**	Kirsten Bärmann-Thümmel
Editor-in-Chief:	Berthold Schwarz	**Cartography:**	Nelles Verlag GmbH
Editors:	Eva Ambros	**Color Separation:**	Priegnitz, München
	Christian Steinmaßl	**Printed by:**	Gorenjski Tisk

No part of this book, not even excerpts, may be reproduced in any form without the express written permission of Nelles Verlag   - S10 -

TABLE OF CONTENTS

HISTORY

TRAVELING IN EGYPT

FEATURES

GUIDELINES

LIST OF MAPS

Note: In some cases the spelling of place names in the maps is not identical with that in the text. For all maps the UN guidelines have been used, whereas in the text the more common English transcription of Arabic names has sometimes been used. In Egypt the English transcription of place names, based on the Egyptian form of Arabic, frequently differs widely from the UN spellings which are based on High Arabic. In city plans the spelling generally conforms to the local Egyptian transcription into English.

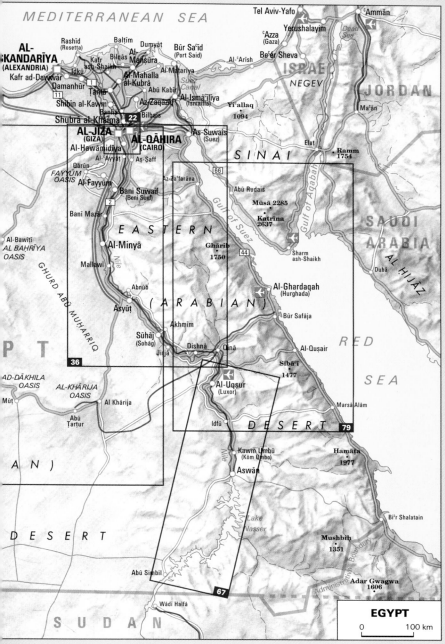

MEDITERRANEAN SEA

Tel Aviv-Yafo
ʿAmmān
Yerushalayim

AL-ISKANDARĪYA
(ALEXANDRIA)

Rashīd
(Rosetta)
Baltīm
Dumyāt
Būr Saʿīd
(Port Said)
ʿAzza
(Gaza)
Beʾér Sheva

Kafr
abū-Shaikh
Idkū
Kafr ad-Dawwār
Al-Mansūra
Al-ʿArish
ISRAEL

Damanhūr
Tanta
Al-Matarīya
NEGEV

Al-Mahalla al-Kubrā
Abū Kabīr
JORDAN

Shibīn al-Kawm
Az-Zaqāzīq
Al-Ismāʿīlīya
(Ismailia)
Yiʾallaq
1094
Maʿān

Banhā
Bilbais

Shubra al-Khaima

AL-JĪZA
(GIZA)
AL-QĀHIRA
(CAIRO)
As-Suwais
(Suez)
Elat
Ramm
1754

Al-Hawāmidīya

Qārūn
Al-ʿAyyāt
Aş-Şaff
Az-Zaʿfarāna
SINAI

FAYYŪM OASIS
Al-Fayyūm
66
Abū Rudais
Mūsā 2285

Banī Suwaif
(Beni Suef)
Katrīna
2637

Banī Mazār

Al-Bawītī
AL BAHRĪYA OASIS
EASTERN
Al-Minyā
Ghārib
1750
44
Sharm ash-Shaikh
Dubā
AL HIJĀZ

GHURD ABŪ MUHARRIQ
Mallawī
SAUDI ARABIA

Abnūb
Al-Ghardaqah
(Hurghada)

Asyūt
(ARABIAN)
Būr Safāja

Akhmīm

EGYPT
Sūhāj
(Sohāg)
Dishnā
Qinā
Al-Qusair
RED

Jirjā
SEA

36
Sibāʿī
1477

AD-DĀKHILA OASIS
AL-KHĀRIJA OASIS
Al-Uqsur
(Luxor)

Mūt
Al Khārija
Marsā ʿAlām

Abū Tartur
Idfū
DESERT
79

(ARABIAN)
Kawm Umbū
(Kōm Ombo)
Hamāta
1977

Aswān

DESERT
Biʾr Shalatain

Lake Nasser
Mushbih
1351

Abū Simbil
Adar Gwagwa
1606

67
Administrative Boundary

Wādī Halfā

SUDAN

EGYPT

0   100 km

The Kingdoms of the Pharaohs

c. 6000 BC Increasing aridity in the Sahara favors the transition to a sedentary lifestyle, the settlement of the oases, the Nile Valley and the Nile Delta.

3500 BC Uniform culture from Nubia to the Nile Delta. Lively communication and joint water administration between the main cities, which were probably organized as city-states.

3050 BC Unification of Upper and Lower Egypt by Menes, founder of the First Dynasty.

Old Kingdom (2715–2192 BC) First cultural flowering under the rulers of the Third to the Sixth Dynasties, who have their seat of power in Memphis.

2697–2677 BC King Djoser (Third Dynasty) has a stepped pyramid built by the architect Imhotep, near present-day Saqqâra.

2641–2521BC Building of the pyramids of Cheops, Khafre and Mykerinos (Fourth Dynasty) near Gîza.

2521–2359 BC Rise of sun worship (Fifth Dynasty).

2259–2195 BC Decline begins during the 66-year reign of Pepi II (Sixth Dynasty).

First Intermediate Period (2192–2040 BC) Famine and civil war cause the state to break up.

Middle Kingdom (2040–1781 BC) King Mentuhotep II (Eleventh Dynasty) restores political unity. A new flowering, regarded as the classical period of Egyptian culture, begins.

1991–1781 BC The Twelfth Dynasty, with several kings named Amenemhet and Sesostris, consolidates the centralized state form and its rule extends beyond the second cataract of the Nile. First ventures into Palestine.

Second Intermediate Period (1781–1550 BC) Alongside the weakening Thirteenth Dynasty lesser kings become established in the Delta (Fourteenth Dynasty). Around 1650 BC the Near Eastern Hyksos (Fifteenth and Sixteenth Dynasties) seize power. The Theban princes of the Seventeenth Dynasty succeed in driving out the Hyksos.

New Kingdom (1550–1080 BC) The new unification ushers in the period of Egypt's greatest power under the Eighteenth to the Twentieth Dynasties. Tuthmosis I (1504–1492 BC) and Tuthmosis III. (1479–1425 BC) extend the kingdom to the Euphrates and far into the Sudan. Capital of the realm is Thebes, the Temple of Amen-Ra is the state temple and the Valley of the Kings becomes the burial place of the Pharaohs.

1479–1457 BC Hatshepsut acts as regent for her stepson, Tuthmosis III, who is a minor, then proclaims herself Pharoah.

1392–1353 BC Peace and prosperity mark the reign of Amenhotep III, but the military and the priesthood increasingly oppose the king.

1353–1337 BC Amenhotep IV–Akhnaton dispenses with the traditional religion and declares Aton to be the only god. The new capital is Armana.

1333–1324 BC Tutankhamen reinstates the old gods and their priests.

Golden lion at a ritual bed, from the Tomb of Tutankhamen.

1279–1213 BC Ramses II holds back the Hittites and becomes a great builder.

1189–1158 BC Ramses III, the last significant king of the New Period, drives away the sea people.

Third Intermediate Period (1080–713 BC): Egypt is again divided into a southern theocracy and the Delta realm, which later splits into principalities.

The Late Period (713–332 BC): After reunification by the Nubian rulers Egypt flourishes one last time under the Twenty-fifth and Twenty-sixth Dynasties.

525–404 BC Egypt is a Province of Persia.

Antiquity and Christianity

332 BC Alexander the Great conquers Egypt.

323 BC Ptolemy receives Egypt after Alexander's death and founds the Ptolemaic Dynasty.

51 BC Cleopatra VII ascends the throne of Egypt.

31 BC Octavian defeats Cleopatra and Marcus Antonius in the sea battle of Actium.

30 BC–395 AD Egypt is a province of the Roman Empire and the "granary" of Rome.

451 AD Council of Chalcedon: The Egyptian Christians separate from the Roman imperial church.

View onto the Sultan Hasan Mosque and the modern city of Cairo.

Under the Banner of Islam

639–642 Islamic conquest of the Land of the Nile.

750–868 Egypt is under the sovereignty of the Abbasid rulers in Baghdad.

868–905 Egypt gains independence under Ahmad Ibn Tûlûn and the Tulunid rulers.

969 The North African Fatimids seize power and found the city of Cairo.

1171 Saladin ends the era of the Fatimids.

1250–1517 Under the Mamelukes Cairo becomes the center of the Arabic-Islamic world.

Modern Age and Present Day

1517 With the absorption into the Ottoman Empire the darkest period of Egyptian history begins, with bloody power struggles.

1798–1801 Napoleon's troops occupy Egypt. Documentation carried out by French scientists leads to the founding of Egyptology.

1805–1848 Muhammad 'Alî, Ottoman governor and viceroy (khedive) is the de facto independent ruler of Egypt. The irrigation system is extended and the cultivation of cotton introduced.

1822 Jean-François Champollion deciphers the hieroglyphics.

1863–1879 Ismâ'îl, Muhammad 'Alî's grandson leads the country into debt and to the edge of bankruptcy through ambitious infrastructure projects and a luxurious lifestyle at his court .

1869 Inauguration of the Suez Canal.

1875 Debts force Ismâ'îl to sell the Suez Canal shares to England.

1882 Revolt of Colonel 'Orabîs. British troops march in to protect the khedive.

1914 Great Britain offically declares Egypt to be a protectorate.

1922 Under King Fu'âd I Egypt obtains independence (in appearance only).

1952 Bloodless coup of the "Free Officers" under Nasser who becomes President in 1953. Land reforms, increase of agricultural yields and industrialization are the chief goals.

1956 The Suez Canal is nationalized by the Egyptian state in order to finance the Aswân High Dam. England, France and Israel occupy the Canal Zone.

1967 Defeat in the Six-Day War against Israel.

1970 Anwâr as-Sâdât succeeds Nasser.

1971 Inauguration of the Aswân High Dam.

1973 Victory in the October War against Israel.

1979 Separate Peace Treaty with Israel, which isolates Egypt in the Arab community.

1981 Murder of Sâdât; Husnî Mubârak succeeds him as President.

1989 Egypt returns to the Arab League.

1991 Participation in the anti-Iraq Gulf War coalition.

1997 More than 60 tourists die in Luxor in an Islamic terror attack.

2000 Thanks to reforms there is huge economic growth. There is also a boom in tourism.

9

Alexandria

ALEXANDRIA - BETWEEN ORIENT AND OCCIDENT

ALEXANDRIA
MONTAZA BAY

****ALEXANDRIA**

"Alexandria is the pearl of the Mediterranean and Egypt's second capital ": thus the Alexandrians enthuse about their home town – along with the hundreds of thousands who flee each summer from the oppressive heat of Cairo to the long sandy beaches of this six million city.

Despite having been repeatedly written off in the past, ****Alexandria** (Arabic: *Al-Iskandarîya)* is once again rising like a phoenix from the ashes; this time as a modern, cosmopolitan, Arabic city with an impressive, if rather faded panorama of tower blocks along the Corniche, its 16-kilometer-long promenade on the sea.

Compared to other cities of the Land of the Nile, Alexandria is fairly young. Alexander the Great founded this city on the Mediterranean on his way back from the oracle of Zeus-Amen in Sîwa in 332 BC. But he was never to see the splendid flourishing of Alexandria, the most famous of all the cities he founded. Not long after his death, it became the capital of Egypt, and simultaneously the majestic residence of the Ptolemaic dynasty.

Preceding pages: Carpet-maker. In the imposing Temple of Abû Simbel. Left: The darker side of the majestic Mosque of Abû al-'Abbas.

Authors of antiquity described ancient Alexandria as a wonderful city with many green parks, a grid of streets through which the cool north wind could blow, and an imposing administrative quarter, the *Regia*, with a palace, official buildings, theaters and the *Museion,* the famous academy with the largest library in the world at the time. But the heart of the city was its unique double harbor, which could be approached from any direction. The *Heptastadion*, a 1300 meter-long artificial dam which divided the natural harbor basin, also served as a causeway to the island of Pharos. There, in 280 BC, Ptolemy II had the famous lighthouse built which was recognised in antiquity as one of the Seven Wonders of the Ancient World.

The ancient city of Alexandria now lies buried under the buildings of the present-day city center or – as spectacular discoveries in the 1990's have revealed – was partially submerged by the sea, as a result of eathquakes and tidal waves. Directly off the coastline French underwater archaeologists discovered granite pillars, statues, chiselled stone blocks and an ancient pavement, which are supposed to have formed a section of the palace of Cleopatra VII (69–30 BC). In this case only a computer-aided reconstruction is possible, but the world-famous *Alexan-*

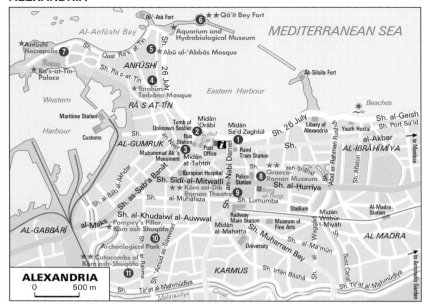

Map labels (from the image):

Ali-Atä Fort · 6 ★★Qâ'it Bey Fort · Al-Anfûshî Bay · Sh. Qasr Ra's at-Tin · MEDITERRANEAN SEA · Aquarium and Hydrobiological Museum · ★Anfûshî Necropolis 7 · 5 ★Abû al-'Abbâs Mosque · al-Akbar · ANFÛSHÎ · Sh. Ra s-at-Tin · As-Silsila Fort · ★Ra's-at-Tîn-Palace · 26 Jul · 4 ★Ibrâhîm Terbâna Mosque · Eastern Harbour · Western · RÂ'S AT-TÎN · ★ Beaches · Maritime Station · Tomb of Unknown Soldier · 2 ★'Orâbî · Midân · Midân Sa'd Zaghlûl · Sh. al-Geish Sh. Port Sa'id · Library of Alexandria · Youth Hostal · Harbour · Sh. · al-Nast · Bus Station · Cecil Sofitel · 1 · al-Akbar · AL-IBRÂHÎMÎYA · Customs · AL-GUMRUK · 3 · Post Office · Raml Tram Station · Sh. · Sh. Abd ar-Rahman Rushdi · Sh. Aflaton · to Muntaza · Muhammad Ali's Monument · Midân at-Tahrîr · Europian Hospital · Sh. ash-Shahid · ★★ Graeco-Roman Museum · 8 · Sh. al-Hurriya · Sh. Sîdi-al-Mitwallî · Police Station · 9 · Sh. an-Nabi Daniel · ★★ Kôm ad-Dik Roman Theatre · al-Muhâfaza · Borg el-Thogr · Sh. Lumumba · AL-GABBÂRÎ · Sh. al-Bâb al-Akhdar · Sh. as-Saba Banat · Sh. al-Khudaiwî al-Auwwal · ★Pompey's Pillar, Kôm ash Shuqâfa · Stadium · Midân Wâbûr l-Miyâh · Al-Madra Station · Railway Main Station · Museum of Fine Arts · AL-MADRA · al-Maks · Midân al-Mahatta · Sh. Muharram Bey · Sh. al-Mâ'mûn · Waggâd · Suez Canal · to Antoniadis Garden · ★★Catacombs of Kôm ash-Shuqâfa · 10 · Archeological Park · Amud as-Sawwari · ar-Rahma · University · KARMUS · Sh. Irfân Bâshâ · to Antoniadis Garden · ALEXANDRIA · 0 · 500 m · 11 · Sh. Tir'at al-Mahmûdiya · Mahmûdiya · Canal · Sh. Tir'at al-Mahmûdiya

---

drian Library* has been awakenened to new life with assistance from UNESCO. In Spring 2001 the complex costing US$ 170 million is to be dedicated, once again making Alexandria an international cultural center after about 1500 years.

The ★City Center and Anfûshî

The pulsing heart of Alexandria lies between **Mîdân al-Mahatta** (Station Square) and the harbors. While the **Eastern Harbor** is today used only by fishing boats and yachts, the **Western Harbor** is increasing in importance for international marine transport. Between the two large harbor basins lies a single spit of land, Anfûshî. This follows the course of the Ptolemaic Heptastadion, which alluvial deposits have widened over the centuries, so that it now joins up with the one-time island of Pharos, forming a strip of settled land.

Right: The Roman Theater of Kôm ad-Dîk is the only one of its kind in Egypt.

A good starting point for a tour of the city and Anfûshî is the **Mîdân Sa'd Zaghlûl** ❶, a wide square on the Corniche, west of which lies the **Cecil Hotel**, a building steeped in tradition. The walking tour will first take you past the ancient columned semicircle of the **Memorial to the Unknown Soldier** ❷ on the Mîdân 'Orâbî, leading onto **Mîdân at-Tahrîr**, which is once again very well maintained. At the center of the square is the **equestrian statue of Muhammad 'Alî** ❸, who inaugurated Alexandria's growth with an ambitious building program. The streets and alleys around the square form a lively shopping district which extends northwards to the bazaars of Anfûshî. Approximately in the center of the spit of land lies the ★**Mosque of Ibrâhîm Terbâna** ❹. Many ancient columns and stone blocks were reused for its construction in the 17th century.

Not far from here, in a large square, is the imposing ★**Mosque of Abû al-'Abbâs** ❺, which was erected in 1943, replacing an older building which had

been destroyed by fire, over the grave of the 13th-century saint. Its filigree façade and the four cupolas ornamented with geometric stone carvings are particularly impressive.

From here is is only a few paces to the ****Fort Qâ'it Bey** ❻ which was built by the Mameluke sultan in the 15th century on the site of the legendary lighthouse. It is worth taking a sightseeing tour of the castle just to see its beautifully renovated rooms and the wonderful view from its battlements. In the ***Hydro-Biological Museum** located next door, the underwater world of the Mediterranean and the Red Sea can be admired.

At the western outskirts of Anfûshî, the ***Necropolis of Anfûshî** ❼ which has two interesting tombs, painted in the mixed Greco-Egyptian style of the second century BC., is worth a visit. In the anterooms, which branch off from a communal atrium, there are wall paintings imitating marble and alabaster tableaux in the style of Pompeian wall decorations, while Egyptian motifs are portrayed in

the burial chambers. Directly beside this, at the western tip of the peninsula, is the ***Palace of Ra's at-Tîn**, built by Muhammad 'Alî. Here the last ruler of his dynasty, King Farûq, signed the declaration of his abdication on July 26, 1952. Unfortunately, its 300 lavishly furnished rooms are not open to the public.

Treasures of Ancient Alexandria

In order to see Alexandria's most significant archeological finds you will need to go to the south of the city center to the ****Museum of Greco-Roman Antiquities** ❽. The museum's exhibits, which date from the time of the Pharaohs to the Christian Era, provide a fine insight into the history of the city and its surroundings. The numismatic collection is particularly famous and also the collection of *Tanagra* figurines: charming small clay figures from the Greek period.

Another interesting site is **Kôm ad-Dîk** ❾ where a superbly-preserved ****Roman Theater** was discovered in

1964, the only one of its kind to be found anywhere in Egypt. It has seating for about 800 spectators in its 12 marble semicircular rows.

The largest site of ancient ruins in Alexandria is the **Archeological Park Kôm ash-Shuqâfa** ⑩, the "hill of potshards" in the southwest of the city. This was once the most important place of worship of the Greco-Egyptian god Serapis. Only a few statues, sphinxes and mud bricks survived the "iconoclasm" of the partiarch Theophilos (AD 391). Today, only the 27-meter-high *Pompey's Pillar** of red granite remains as a landmark of the Serapis temple. This pillar was probably erected in honor of Emperor Diocletian in the year 297 AD. It owes its present name to Pompey's tomb, which was believed to have been situated here.

A few hundred meters farther south you come to the ****Catacombs of Kôm ash-Shuqâfa** ⑪, an unusually fine example of a Roman burial complex dating

Above: The palace of Montâza.

from the first and second centuries AD. You descend a spiral staircase down to the three levels of the underground chambers, of which the burial chapel is decorated in a delightful combination of Egyptian architecture and motifs along with stylistic elements of the Greco-Roman period.

MONTAZA BAY

The small **Bay of Montâza** was popular with the khedives and kings of the 19th and 20th centuries, who built their summer residences in a well-kept park with shady palm groves. "Alexandria's Neuschwanstein," with its playful architecture, is a fine **Neo-Renaissance palace**. Unfortunately, the interior is not open for public viewing. During the Nasser era, the **Palestine Hotel** was built next to it, whose functional, rather than beautiful architecture is compensated for by its splendid setting on the bay. Next to Montâza Bay, **Ma'mûra beach** stretches to the east, as far as Abû Qîr.

ALEXANDRIA (☎ 03)

Alexandria by night and day, which is a brochure containing important addresses and useful information, is available in most hotels and can also be obtained from the **State Tourist Office**. Head office: at Mîdân Sa'd Zaghlûl, Raml Station, tel. 484338. Further branches are located at the airport, port and main train station.

ARRIVAL: Some international **airlines** offer direct routes, and *Egypt Air* services the Cairo–Alexandria route several times daily.

Trains as well as **buses** operated by *West Delta Bus Company* and *Superjet* run almost hourly between Alexandria (Raml bus station: Md. Sa'd Zaghlûl) and Cairo (bus station: for the time being at Md. Turgumân near the main bus station, otherwise 'Abd al-Mun'im Riyâd by the Ramses Hilton). Tickets for luxury buses operated by *Superjet* should be obtained in advance at the ticket kiosk at the bus station.

Alexandria's west port is now only approached by **cruise liners**, meaning that a ferry service connecting Europe is no longer available.

In Alexandria there are innumerable hotels of all categories. Yet accommodation required in high season (July/August) should be booked well in advance. More simple accommodation and pensions are usually closed from October to May. Hotels located directly beside the sea are those along the Corniche, which is called Sh. 26th July in the area around the east port, and east of this as fas as Montâza-Park it is known as Sh. al-Geish. If you want to be centrally located and have a view of the sea, try the area around Mîdân Sa'd Zaghlûl and the Raml station.

★★★ **Montazah Sheraton**, Al-Montâza, tel. 5480550, fax 5401331. **Helnan Palestine**, Al-Montâza, tel. 5474033, fax 5473378. **Ramada Renaissance**, 544 Sh. al-Geish, tel. 5490935, fax 5497690. **Sofitel Cecil**, Md. Sa'd Zaghlûl, tel. 4837173, fax 4836401. **Salamlek Hotel**, Montâza Park, tel. 5477999, fax 5464408.

★★ **Alexandria Hotel**, 23 Md. an-Nasr, tel. 4837694/-97, fax 4823113. **Delta**, 14 Sh. Champollion, Mazarita, tel. 4829053, fax 4825630. **El-Haram**, 162 Sh. al-Geish, tel. 5464059, fax 5464578. **Maamura Palace**, Al-Ma'mûra, tel. 5473108, fax 5473108. **Mecca**, 44 Sh. al-Geish, tel. 5973925, fax 5969935. **Metropole**, 52 Sh. Sa'd Zaghlûl, tel. 4821466/67, fax 4822040. **Plaza**, 394 Sh. al-Geish, tel. 5878714/15, fax 5875399. **San Giovanni**, 205 Sh. al-Geish, tel. 5467774/75, fax 5464408. **Windsor**, 17 Sh. ash-Shuhadâ', Raml, tel. 4808256, fax 4809090.

★ **Holiday**, 6 Md. 'Orâbî, tel. 801559. **New Capri**, 23 Sh. al-Mîna ash-Sharqîya, Raml, tel. 809310. **Swiss Cottage**, 347 Sh. al-Geish, tel. 5875886, fax 5870455. **Nobel**, 152 Sh. al-Geish, tel. 5464845, fax 5457488. **Sea Star**, 25 Sh. Amîn Fakhrî, Raml, tel. 4832388. **Union**, 164 Sh. 26th July, tel. 4807312.

YOUTH HOSTELS: **Youth Hostel**, 13 Sh. Port Said, Shatbî, tel. 5975459.

Alexandria is *the* town for seafood fans. As well as the restaurants in all the luxury hotels, the following are recommended:

FISH: **Tikka Grill**, Sh. 26th July. **Darwish**, Sh. 26th July, Raml. **Santa Lucia**, Sh. Safîya Zaghlûl. **El-Saraya**, Saba Pasha, Sh. al-Geish. **San Giovanni**, 205 Sh. al-Geish. **International Seafood Restaurant**, 808 Sh. al-Geish, Al-Montâza. **Zephyrion**, Abû Qîr (east of Alexandria). **Sea Gull**, Sh. 'Agamî, Al-Maks (suburb west of Alexandria).

ORIENTAL / INTERNATIONAL: **Athineos**, Md. Raml. **Al-Ekhlass**, 49 Sh. Safîya Zaghlûl. **Sokrat**, Sh. Iskander al-akbar, Shatbî. **Taverna**, Raml station (on the ground floor is an oriental snack bar, on the first floor is a small restaurant).

CAFÉS: **Brazilian Coffee Store**, Sh. Sa'd Zaghlûl. **Pastroudis**, 39 Sh. Al-Hurrîya. **Trianon**, Md. Sa'd Zaghlûl.

NIGHT CLUBS: Music and belly-dancing (dinner is obligatory!) available in the hotels **Montazah Sheraton, Plaza, Sofitel Cecil** and **San Giovanni**.

DISCOTHEK: In the **Ramada Renaissance hotel**, closed Mondays.

Fort Qâ'it Bey, daily 8 am-5 pm, Fri 8-11:30 am, 1:30-5 pm. **Kôm ad-Dîk**, Sh. Abd al-Mun'im, daily 9 am-4 pm. **Museum of Greco-Roman Antiquities**, Sh. al-Hurrîya, Sat-Thur 9 am-4 pm, Fri 9 am-12 pm, 2-4 pm; the entrance ticket is also valid for the necropolises of Anfûshî and Kôm ash-Shuqâfa. **Nekropolis of Anfûshi**, daily 9 am-4 pm. **Kôm ash-Schûqafa**, daily 9 am-4 pm.

University Hospital, Shatbî, tel. 4201573. **Italian Hospital**, Al-Hadra, tel. 4221458. A 24-hour pharmacy is located in the city center: **Sa'd Zaghlûl Pharmacy**, Md. al-Manshîya.

CITY TRANSPORTATION: The **group taxi** stand for trips to Alexandria is located in Cairo at the Mîdân al-Qulâlî, near the main train station.

Inner city traffic is very much dominated by **trams**. From Raml station (*Mahattat ar-Raml*) on Md. Sa'd Zaghlûl in the city center, there are tram services to almost all the major sights: **Nr. 2**: Raml station – main train station – Pompey's Pillar; **Nr. 15**: Raml station – Sh. Ahmad 'Orâbî – Anfûshî – Ra's at-Tîn.

Bus Nr's. 735, 736 and **725** run from Md. Sa'd Zaghûl along the Corniche as far as Al-Montâza.

Alexandria

CAIRO

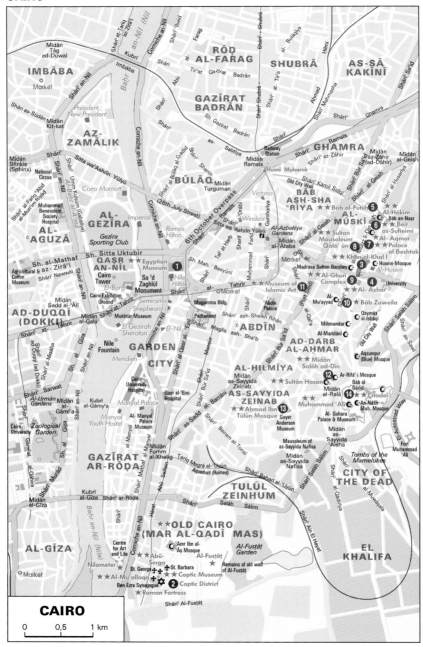

CAIRO AND THE PYRAMIDS

CAIRO
OLD CAIRO
ISLAMIC OLD TOWN
PYRAMIDS OF GÎZA
NECROPOLIS OF SAQQÂRA
MEMPHIS

**CAIRO

"The Mother of all Cities" – that is how the famous Arab traveler Ibn Battûta described Cairo in the 14th century – a distinction which still applies to the modern capital of Egypt. For **Cairo ❶** (Arabic: *Al-Qâhira*) is not only the largest city in Africa – with an estimated population of between 13 and 15 million, and the intellectual center of the Arab world – it is also an unbelievable symbiosis of all conceivable modern ways of life. The dark side of this sparkling microcosm cannot be overlooked, of course, but the joy of life and unshakable humor of the inhabitants of this metropolis are almost irrepressible, even in the face of the difficult living conditions in the hopelessly overpopulated city.

In 1969, Cairo's 1,000th birthday was celebrated – a modest claim which only one of the oldest cultures on earth can allow itself to make. While Al-Qâhira, the namesake of modern Cairo, was not actually founded until the 10th century, a long series of famous cities preceded it: the residence of the Pharaohs, **Memphis**; the Greco-Roman settlement and fortress city of **Babylon**, which was later inhabited by Christians; **Fustât**, which was founded by the Arab conqueror of Egypt, 'Amr Ibn al-'Âs in the seventh century

;**Al-Qatâ'i'**, the seat of government of Ahmad Ibn Tûlûn who ruled Egypt in the ninth century. Finally in the year 969, Gôhar, the commander of the Fatimids conquered all of Egypt on behalf of his caliph, Mu'izz li-Dîn-Illah, and laid the foundations for a new city: **Al-Qâhira**, "The Victorious," named after the planet Mars (Arabic: *Al-Qâhir),* which could be seen in the sky at the time when the city was founded.

Not until Saladin seized power, in 1171, were the gates of Al-Qâhira thrown open to everyone, and around this center the splendid old town of present-day Cairo developed.

During the Mameluke era, which lasted from 1250 to 1517, Cairo's star shone brighter than ever. The sultans, always fond of ostentation, made huge profits in their trade with Asia and decorated their capital with the most beautiful buildings.

With the Ottoman invasion of 1517, Cairo became nothing more than an insignificant provincial capital. Many traces of Turkish rule can be found in the architecture of the city, but by and large these traces are unimportant. The new rise in fortunes began with Muhammad 'Alî (1805-48). His Alabaster Mosque in the Citadel was only the beginning. The construction of the Suez Canal com-

pletely changed the face of Cairo. In order to present the illustrious guests at the inauguration celebrations in 1869 with a glittering metropolis, new neighborhoods were built in European style, in a great flurry of activity. A wide ceremonial street was built to Gîza and the pyramids, and to the **Mena House**Palace Hotel (see map on page 22) and another straight through the old town to the Citadel.

The European style continued to characterize the architecture in the city center of Cairo, on the island of Al-Gazîra and on the banks of the Nile.

President Nasser later also chose this area to be the setting for the representative buildings of the young Arab Republic of Egypt, whose architectural symbol is the 187-meter-high Cairo Tower.

In the north of the **Mîdân at-Tahrîr**, the center of modern Cairo, is the classi-cal-style building of the Egyptian Museum.

**The Egyptian Museum

The sheer number of exhibits in the **The Egyptian Museum ❶ (approximately 120,000) means that it is almost impossible to see everything. *The Official Catalogue of the Egyptian Museum* will serve as an excellent guide, taking you through the main works of art in chronological order. A separate ticket must be purchased in order to visit the Hall of Mummies.

The rooms on the **Ground Floor** exhibit a splendid collection of ancient Egyptian sculpture and stonemasonry and – starting with rooms 43 and 47 – form a guided tour clockwise through five millenia.

The **Upper Floor** contains several almost perfectly preserved tomb finds, a collection of ancient Egyptian jewelry and papyrus with religious text. The main features, however, are the **Hall of Mummies** in which the mummies of fa-

Above: Looking with awe and admiration at Tutankhamen's gold coffin from the Valley of the Kings (Egyptian Museum). Far right: A Coptic monk.

mous kings, such as Ramses II and his father Seti I, as well as of other kings and queens, are kept, and furthermore the **Burial Treasures of Tutankhamen** which is to be found in the gallery rooms of the right wing and of the back lateral tract. The tomb was discovered in 1922 by Howard Carter in the Valley of Kings. Of the more than 3,500 objects found in the tomb, 1,700 of them can be seen here.

★★OLD CAIRO

In the south of the city, across from the Nile island of Ar-Rôda, lies **★★Old Cairo**. This is the historical core of Cairo, the site of the first Arabic city to be founded in Egypt, **Fustât**, which grew up alongside the Greco-Roman town of Babylon.

The walls of the Roman fortress of Babylon have been partially preserved and surround Cairo's oldest quarter: the **Coptic Quarter** ❷ where the beautiful churches and the Coptic Museum are among the most unusual places of interest in this city which otherwise owes more to the influence of Islam.

The **★Roman Fortress** once lay directly on the Nile, the course of which, in ancient times, ran about 400 meters farther east. Harbors found six meters underground show that Babylon was once an important center of trade. The fortress itself dates back to the time of Augustus (30 BC). It was completely renovated under Trajan (98–117) and restored once more in the time of the Byzantine Emperor Arcadius (395–408).

The Church of the Holy Virgin is called **★★Al-Mu'allaqa** – the Hanging One – in common parlance, because it was built over the Roman southwestern gate. Nothing remains from the fourth century when it was founded, and only a few remains from its many renovations and restorations until the 18th century can still be seen. The church was given its present form in 1775. Already at its entrance you

will be enchanted: the Baroque-style façade, with a wide stairway leading up to it, rises over a small palm garden. Behind the covered forecourt you come upon a pretty inner courtyard with a fountain. The interior of this splendid church is divided assymetrically by three arcades, formed by ancient white marble columns, into the nave and the side aisles. As in all Coptic churches, the chancel itself is also divided into three parts: the chapels of St. George (left), Jesus Christ (middle) and John the Baptist (right) are separated from the prayer room by a magnificent iconostasis of ebony, inlaid with ivory, which dates from the 13th century. The icons above the iconostasis date back to the 18th century. In front of it is a dainty marble pulpit from the 11th century. You can enter the chapel of Takla Hajmanot, one of the most famous Coptic saints (13th century), and the baptistry from the right-hand aisle. You will discover a wonderful view of the walls of the southern ramparts through a glass window in the floor.

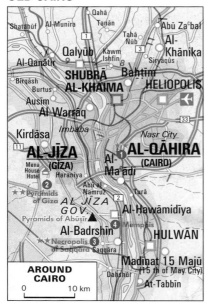

AROUND CAIRO

0   10 km

The **Coptic Museum** houses a unique collection of Coptic art treasures which document the stylistic development from what were, at the beginning, Hellenic-Roman art forms to more Byzantine-influenced icon paintings, and later to ornamental art showing strong Islamic influences. The beautiful weavings that can be seen here represent a high point in Coptic art.

From the Museum Garden, to the right of the ticket-office, a small lane leads directly to the center of the Coptic Quarter.

After a few paces you come to a second church, to which a visit should not be missed: the **Abû Serga Church**, dedicated to the martyrs Sergius and Bacchus. The present building dates only from the 10th and 11th centuries, and was erected under the Fatimids, but the founding of the church probably dates from the fifth century; the Holy Family is supposed to have lived at the spot where the pres-

Right: The Al-Azhar Mosque is the center of learning of Sunni Islam.

ent-day crypt now disappears into the ground water. The interior of the church is dark and exudes an aura of mystery and secrecy. Its architecture is a classic example of an early Christian basilica, with a raised nave and two side aisles. The high altar, which stands beneath a wooden dome-shaped baldachin, can best be admired from the chapel of St. George to the left. The chapel to the right of the inner sanctum is dedicated to St. Michael. Here, too, the entire altar area lies behind the ebony wall of an iconostasis which is decorated with ivory incrustations and carvings.

**THE ISLAMIC OLD CITY

Of the three fairy-tale cities of the Islamic Orient – Cairo, Damascus and Baghdad – the Egyptian metropolis was the only one to remain undamaged by the devastation caused by Mongol attacks, and was therefore able to retain its medieval **Islamic old city**, which in spite of many restoration projects is falling into an increasing state of disrepair.

In the area where Al-Qâhira was founded as a Fatimid residence in 969, the large bazaar quarter is located. The **Khân al-Khalîlî** ❸ is the most famous, but not the only *sûq* (Arabic for bazaar). Immediately beside it is the *Sûq an-Nahâssîn*, the market of the coppersmiths who still make the minaret tips today. But the old bazaar divisions according to wares and guilds are no longer so strictly adhered to. And so you will sometimes see a spice merchant next to a butcher, or a shoemaker in the middle of the cloth market.

The whole shopping paradise stretches in a maze of alleys on both sides of the busy main street Sh. al-Azhar. The real **Khân al-Khalîlî** begins opposite the Al-Azhar Mosque on the Mîdân Husein. A good point of reference, in case you should lose your way in the Khân al-Khalîlî, is the minaret of the **Husein**

Mosque (closed to non-Muslims!) which is shaped like a pencil and can be seen for quite some distance.

Although there are plenty of souvenirs on offer, the Khân al-Khalîlî is in no way a bazaar strictly for tourists. The inhabitants of Cairo still buy their jewelry here, and the main axis **Sh. al-Gôhar al-Qâ'id**, locally called *Sh. Muskî* is like one huge department store where you can buy everything from aluminium pots to bridal gowns.

★★Al-Azhar Mosque

Only a few buildings today reflect the splendor of the Cairo at the time of the Fatimids. The **★★Al-Azhar Mosque** ❹ is one of these.

Until 1961 theology, the Islamic sciences, Islamic Law (Arabic: *Shar'îa*) and Arabic were the only subjects taught at the university. Today, there are additional faculties for economics and business, medicine, pharmacology, engineering, agriculture, the natural sciences and the arts. But even those who choose a secular subject of study are obliged to attend lectures and take exams in theology and Islamic law. More than 100,000 students are taught by around 4,000 professors here. Since 1964, the doors of the Islamic University have also been open to women.

You enter the mosque, which is dominated by three minarets, through the **Barbers' Gate** (where the students' heads were, according to tradition, once shaved). To the left is the **Library**, with its 60,000 manuscripts. This was erected with the building on the right as a *madrasa* (mosque school) in the 14th century. Behind a portal with beautiful wood carvings the central court opens out. This dates from the 10th-century Fatimid building. The decoration of the colonnade, with its medals and arched paneling, however, dates from the 12th century. The portal itself and the minaret

above it were built by Sultan Qâ'it Bey (1469). The covered prayer room, a giant hypostyle hall, joins the court. The prayer niche in the central nave marks the original division of the five-aisled hall as it was built by Gôhar. It was only in the 18th century that it was extended by a further four aisles to the east. Here you can still sometimes see students sitting in semicircles at the feet of their teachers, as has been done for almost a thousand years. Otherwise, today almost all the lectures take place in the modern university buildings.

★★Between Bâb al-Futûh and Bâb Zuweila

The most beautiful buildings in the heart of the bazaar quarters can all be found on the **Sh. Mu'izz li-Dîn-Illah**, once a majestic 15-meter-wide boulevard at the heart of the Fatimid's palace city, Al-Qâhira. In 1087, Vizier Badr al-Gamâlî had a new and bigger city wall built, the first monumental stone contruction of the Islamic era of Egypt. Here, in the northern part of the wall, the two large gates **Bâb an-Nasr** and ****Bâb al-Futûh** ❺ have been preserved, along with a 600 meter-long section of the wall. This borders directly on the ****Al-Hâkim Mosque** (1013) of which there is a good view from Bâb al-Futûh, the "Gate of Conquests" (staircase beside the gate). Restoration work carried out on the mosque was financed by an Ismailite sect from India, and since its completion the mosque of the Fatimid caliph once again shines in all its former glory. White, shimmering alabaster paving stones cover the square of the broad courtyard which is bordered by covered arcades several aisles wide.

A few steps further, on the left-hand side, in the little side street Darb alAsfar, you will discover one of the finest private Ottoman-era residences in all Cairo: the ****Beit as-Suheimî** ❻, (17th century).

Returning to Sh. Mu'izz li-Dîn-Illah keep a look out on the left-hand side of the street for the beautiful ornate façade of the ***Al-Aqmar Mosque**, built in 1125. A little further on, another street joins Sh. Mu'izz li-Dîn-Illah at a sharp angle from the north. The building on the corner of the two streets is the charming ****Well House of 'Abd ar-Rahmân Kathkûda** (built in 1744). A *sabîl kuttâb*, as this combination of a public well (situated on the first floor) and a Koran school (on the second floor) is called, was the most popular form of religious endowment during the Ottoman period. The interior of the well house is decorated with blue Syrian tiles.

Just past the well house is the **** Palace of Amîr Beshtak** ❼ (1339). This impressive building with a magnificent banqueting room is one of the very few examples of Mameluke secular architecture and was beautifully restored in the 1980's

Right: View over Cairo's medieval Islamic old town.

by means of German-Egyptian cooperation. (The entrance to the palace can be found on the neighboring side street.)

Something definitely not to be missed is a visit to the interior of the ****Mausoleum of Sultan Qalâ'ûn** ❽, which the ruler had built, along with a madrasa and a hospital, from 1284 to 1285.

Inside the mausoleum is the largest ornamental open-work carved wooden screen in Cairo. It is 17 x 4 meters large and surrounds the sarcophagi of the Sultan and his son Muhammad an-Nâsir. The central cupola rises like a baldachin on four pillars and four massive columns, the arcades of which are decorated with beautiful plasterwork and join together to form a graceful octagonal ensemble. The walls are ornamentally lined with different-colored marble panels, stone paneling with polychromatic inlays, and golden inscriptions. The prayer niche is inlaid with colorful, gleaming mosaics and divided by rows of small alabaster pillars.

Across the main traffic artery, Sh. al-Azhar, the Sh. Mu'izz li-Dîn-Illah continues southwards through the colorful cloth market. The buildings of the ****Al-Ghûrî Complex** ❾ form a kind of monumental entrance to it: the **madrasa** on the right and the **Mausoleum of Sultan Al-Ghûrî** (1503-05) on the left. The distinguishing characteristic of the Madrasa of Al-Ghûrî is its 65-meter-high minaret with its five miniature cupolas.

The interior rooms are splendid, with the richly decorated arched keel construction of the four halls around the inner courtyard, and the fine east wall with its prayer niche. The mausoleum opposite nowadays houses an adult education center. Make sure you take a look at the cupola room to the right of the entrance, which has been tastefully renovated and is now used as a library.

The ***Bâb Zuweila** ❿ at the end of the Sh. Mu'izz li-Dîn-Illah can be seen from quite a distance; it is one of three of the

original 60 city gates of the Fatimid wall that are still standing. Nowadays it is crowned by the two minarets of the **★Al-Mu'ayyad Mosque**. Together they make up an imposing architectural scene, chosen by the Mameluke sultan (1412–21) for his mosque. The portal of the prayer room is decorated with stalactites, arabesques and inscriptions from the Koran, and is sealed off by a heavy bronze gate.

If you turn right after passing through the city gate, you will only be a short distance from the **Mîdân Ahmad Mâhir**, with the **★★Museum of Islamic Art ⓫**. Generously laid out, the museum exhibits represent a wide selection from the enormous store of more than 80,000 objects, mostly from Egypt, but also from Turkey and Persia, which can be seen here. Alongside many beautiful architectural exhibits, the museum contains wonderful mosque lamps and Koran stands, furniture with valuable inlays, brass creations, an exquisite polychromatic marble well, *mashrabîya* work, ceramics, and a rich

and varied collection of carpets situated on the upper floor.

Around the Citadel

The perfectly circular **★★Mîdân Salâh ad-Dîn ⓬** is an excellent starting point for a visit to the Citadel and the surrounding mosques.

The best place to begin the tour is at the **★★Madrasa of Sultan Hasan**, considered to be a masterpiece of Mameluke architecture. The monumental portal is decorated with a cascade of stone stalactites and leads into a high anteroom. On the other side of a dark corridor there is a splendid inner courtyard. Its square is surrounded by four vaulted halls, the *îwâns*.

Each of the îwâns was reserved for one of the four orthodox law schools of Sunni Islam, and in each of these halls the law scholars taught their students according to their tradition. Behind them are several storeys of living and studying rooms for the teachers and students. The extrava-

gant splendor of this mosque is consistently tasteful – whether it be the polychrome marble inlay of the floor or the îwâns; or the shining gold mosaic of the prayer niche; or the massive bronze portals, covered with silver and gold, which lead into the mausoleum of the sultan. The decorative frieze, with Kufic inscriptions from the Koran, is particularly impressive. The burial chamber, covered by a dome, contains the sarcophagus of the sultan – which was never used – and a beautiful stand for holding the Koran.

Before climbing to the Citadel, though, you should make a visit to the **Ibn Tûlûn Mosque** ⓭ (AD 876–79) located nearby. The center of the spacious courtyard of the Ibn Tûlûn Mosque is the well house, which when being restored in 1296 was completely rebuilt. A colonnade with three aisles, and five aisles in the main wing, leads around the courtyard. The most splendid of the six prayer niches is

Above: Impressive ensemble at the Mîdân Salâh ad-Dîn .

shaped like an apse, and is adorned with marble inlays and gold mosaics. The interlacing filigree ornamentation of the pointed-arch arcades and the 128 different carved windows represent an impressive display of the stonemason's skill. Of particular interest is the spiral minaret: it is 40 meters high and reminiscent of the minaret of the great mosque in Samarra in Iraq, the architecture of which Ibn Tûlûn emulated for his own structure.

If you want to go from the Mîdân Salâh ad-Dîn up to the **★★Citadel** ⓮ on foot, you should take the street leading eastwards to the New Gate, the **Bâb al-Gadîd**, which was built under Muhammad 'Alî, and there turn right into the fortress. Sultan Saladin began the construction of the Citadel in the year 1176, but it was only completed 45 years later by his nephew Al-Kâmil.

The **★★Muhammad 'Alî Mosque** is the landmark of the Citadel as well as of Cairo. This was built by the sultan in 1830 in the Turkish style. It takes its second name, the "Alabaster Mosque," from

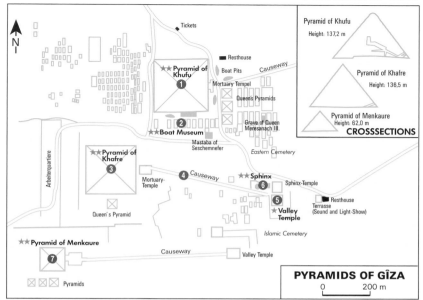

its rich covering of this valuable stone. The domed main building with the sultan's mausoleum is joined to the inner courtyard, which is surrounded by columned arcades.

**PYRAMIDS OF GÎZA

To the west of Cairo, where the Sahara borders the Nile Valley, is the plateau of Gîza. Here you will find some of the most famous constructions in human history: the **Pyramids of Gîza ❷**, built by the kings Cheops (or Khufu), Khafre and Mykerinos in the middle of the third millenium BC.

The methods and techniques used in the building of the pyramids still puzzle scientists today. Because the written sources of the ancient Egyptians reveal nothing on this matter, one has to resort to theories, and there are many of those. Recent research has come up with the following likely picture of the building of the two great pyramids in Gîza. The building site was levelled around an out-

cropping rock core, and a flat plateau was thus created upon which the ground plan of the pyramid was marked out. After the underground burial chambers had been dug, horizontal stone layers were built up to form the solid core. The shining white limestone covering was put in place at the same time. The stones for the core came from the immediate surroundings, while the covering blocks of white limestone were brought from Tura on the eastern bank of the Nile; those of Cheops' pyramid came from almost all the limestone quarries in the country. With the aid of rollers and sleds the huge blocks, which had an average weight of two to three tons, were transported on ramps. There is quite a bit of debate today as to what these ramps would have looked like. Most recently, scholars have tended to favor the opinion that a ramp was leaned against one side of the pyramid and could be extended as progress in height was made. But it must have given way to steps for the last third of the construction. There the architects must have employed the lifting devices of which Herodotus speaks. He also speaks of up to 100,000 people having worked on the pyramid, although modern scholars have calculated that about 20,000 Egyptians probably worked on it for 20 years. Of these, 5,000 were specialists, the rest simple laborers.

The pyramids stand tall on the Plateau of Gîza, surrounded by the tombs of the royal family and high officials. The largest of all is the **Pyramid of Cheops** ❶. Originally, it had side lengths of 230.4 meters and a height of 146.6 meters. But because, like all pyramids, it has been used as a stone quarry since the Middle Ages, the Pyramid of Cheops today only has a base length of 227.5 meters, and with an angle of incline of 51°50'40" it is about 137 meters high. The layout of the pyramid's ground plan was aligned to the four points of the compass, so that the diagonal is precisely northeast-southwest. The average deviation is only 3'40". More than two million cut stone blocks make up the enormous Pyramid of Cheops, which is almost 2.6 million cubic meters in volume. The original 210 stone layers, of which 201 remain today, were covered with granite at the bottom and fine white limestone above that.

The entrance on the north side of the pyramid is covered with huge gabled blocks. It remained hidden beneath the stone covering until the Middle Ages. Today, you enter the monument through a hole made by grave robbers some meters deeper. The passageway to the 35-meter-deep underground **Rock Chamber** is closed to visitors, as is the passage to the so-called **Queen's Chamber** which branches off the foot of the Great Gallery.

The monumental architecture of the **Great Gallery** (47 x 1 – 2 x 8.5 meters) is overwhelming. The walls of polished limestone are covered by a grandiose ceiling in the form of a corbeled vault.

Right: In front of the pyramids of Kings Cheops, Khafre and Mykernios in Gîza.

The niches above the banquettes on both sides served as anchors for granite blocks which were released after the burial in order to finally seal the system of corridors. At the end of the gallery you come to a low passageway which was once closed by four fallen stones, only one of which can still be seen today. Behind this the imposing **Burial Chamber** of the king (10.5 x 5.2 x 5.8 meters) opens out to a height of nearly 43 meters. Its walls are paneled with pink granite and it contains the empty shell of the granite sarcophagus. The mummy of Cheops has never been found.

To the east of the pyramids once stood the great **Mortuary Temple**, of which only some of the black basalt paving stones have been preserved. The grounds of the Mortuary Temple were flanked by two 50 meter-long pits for the barques in which the Sun God made his journey to heaven according to ancient Egyptian belief. On the south side of the Pyramid of Cheops are two more of the total of five boat pits. In one of them, in 1954, a fully preserved cedar boat was found in 1,224 separate pieces.

Directly above the site of the find, a **Boat Museum** ❷ was built to accommodate the 43-meter-long and almost five-meter-wide boat, in which it is presumed the grave furnishings, or perhaps even the king himself, were probably brought to the pyramid.

The **Pyramid of Khafre** ❸ is recognizable by the well-preserved limestone covering at its tip. This and the somewhat steeper angle of incline of 53°10' gives you the impression that Khafre's pyramid is larger than that of his father Cheops. In truth, though, it is a little smaller, with a base length of 215.25 meters and an original height of 143.5 meters (today 136.5 meters). The covering of the two bottom layers was of granite, as in the Pyramid of Cheops, and above that came a coating of gleaming white limestone. At no other pyramid has the funeral complex been so

well-preserved. On the east side of the pyramid, which in ancient times was surrounded by a 10-meter-wide covered walkway, are the mighty blocks of the **Mortuary Temple**. A **ramp** ❹, almost 500 meters long and shaped as a corridor with limestone walls, once joined it to the ***Valley Temple** ❺ on the border of the fertile lands. The corridor to the pyramid causeway leads off to the right inside the temple. From there you get a good view of the ruins of its temple and of the 57-meter-long, 20-meter-high figure of the ****Great Sphinx** ❻. For a long time it was thought that this monumental stone creature, with the body of a lion and the face of a man, was a representation of King Khafre. Now it is thought that it was the guardian of a sun temple which stood at the eastern corner of the immense complex of the great Pyramid of Cheops.

It was probably due to the rise of the cult of the sun during the Fourth Dynasty that Khafre's son and heir erected a considerably more modest tomb for himself. The ****Pyramid of Mykerinos** ❼, with

side lengths of 102.2 x 104.6 meters and an angle of incline of around 51°, is "only" about 66 meters high. The granite covering of the lower third of the pyramid can still be seen. Above that the pyramid was covered with white limestone. In 1837, the remains of a mummy (probably that of King Mykerinos) were found when the burial chamber was opened. A basalt sarcophagus was also found, but it was lost when the ship transporting it to England sank. On the south side of the pyramid are three smaller secondary pyramids; on the east side the remains of a mortuary temple and of the causeway can be made out.

THE **NECROPOLIS OF SAQQÂRA

A field of pyramids stretches for several kilometers along the edge of the desert to the south of Gîza. The largest and most important city of the dead is the ****Necropolis of Saqqâra** ❸, 15 kilometers away, which from the beginning of

SAQQÂRA

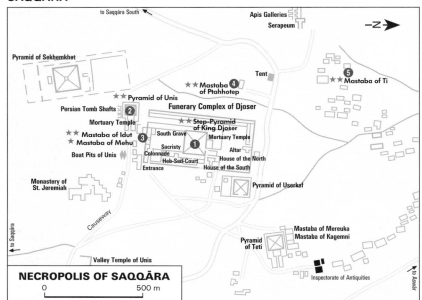

to Saqqâra South
Apis Galleries
Serapeum
—Z→

Pyramid of Sekhemkhet

Tent

★★Mastaba of Ptahhotep ④

⑤ ★★Mastaba of Ti

★★Pyramid of Unis

Funerary Complex of Djoser

Persian Tomb Shafts ②

Mortuary Temple

★★Step-Pyramid of King Djoser

★★Mastaba of Idut
★ Mastaba of Mehu

South Grave ③ Mortuary Temple

Boat Pits of Unis

Sacristy ①
Colonnade
Heb-Sed-Court
Entrance

Altar
House of the North
House of the South

Monastery of St. Jeremiah

Pyramid of Userkaf

Causeway

Mastaba of Mereuka
Mastaba of Kagemni

Pyramid of Teti

to Saqqâra

Valley Temple of Unis

NECROPOLIS OF SAQQÂRA
0   500 m

Inspectorate of Antiquities

to Aswân

the First Dynasty onwards served as a cemetery for nearby Memphis. Fifteen kings of the Old Kingdom, countless princes and princesses, and high officials and priests from all other epochs of Egyptian history had their tombs erected here.

Even from a distance, the **★★Stepped Pyramid of King Djoser ①** dominates the necropolis. The tomb of this Third Dynasty king (c. 2700 BC) stands at the center of an architectural complex which was once surrounded by a 544 x 277-meter-long wall. Fourteen portals are integrated in the niches of this imposing limestone wall, but only the one in the southeast corner actually opens into the entrance passage.

The **Pyramid** rises to a height of 60 meters, over a ground base of 121 x 109 meters, in six sloping steps. But it was not planned to be a construction of such massive proportions from the beginning: at first a simple single-stepped mastaba was

erected over the underground burial chamber, which, after several extensions, developed into a monumental six-stepped construction. The true king's tomb (not accessible to the public) is a chamber, walled in by huge granite blocks, at the bottom of a 28-meter-deep vertical shaft. Forty thousand valuable stone vessels were discovered in the subterranean galleries.

On the north side of the pyramid is the **Statue Chamber** with the famous seated figure of Djoser (the original of which is in the Egyptian Museum).

The **★★Pyramid of Unas ②** is situated in the southwestern corner of the Djoser complex. Unas was the last king of the Fifth Dynasty. The monument, which once stood 44 meters tall, now seems more like a heap of rubble. But a visit to its burial chamber should not be missed. The walls of the anteroom and of the burial chamber are decorated over and over with *Pyramid Texts* – a collection of ritual sayings, magic formulae and prayers which were intended to safeguard

Right: The toppled Colossus of Ramses II in the open-air museum in Memphis.

the continued existence of the dead ruler and to guarantee his acceptance into the circle of gods.

Here in Saqqâra, the block-shaped mastabas of the nobility are also grouped like settlements around the royal pyramids. The walls were richly decorated with scenes depicting earthly life, such as working in the fields, fishing and hunting, dancing and playing, artisans busy in their workshops, and many other things.

The **Mastaba of Idut ❸**, a princess of the Sixth Dynasty, lies to the south of the Djoser area. Five of the total of 10 chambers of her tomb are decorated with colorful relief cycles, the other rooms were built as storerooms. In the neighboring *Mastaba of Mehu, a vizier of the Sixth Dynasty, the wonderful wall paintings have been just as well preserved.

To the northwest of the Stepped Pyramid of Djoser is the **Mastaba of Ptahhotep ❹** (Fifth Dynasty). The small cultic chapel here is a high point in any visit to Saqqâra. Furthermore, the unfinished reliefs decorating the entrance

corridor give you a good idea of the stonemasons' technique.

Northwest of here you can find the **Mastaba of Ti ❺** (Fifth Dynasty) – which lies hidden in a sand basin – you will find some of the finest examples of ancient Egyptian reliefs. On the walls of the sacrificial hall is the complete cycle of cultivation, from sowing to harvesting (over the entrance and the east wall, left). Scenes such as boat building, statue sculpting and carpentry stretch from the east wall to the south wall. You can see the Ka statue of Ti through slits in the wall (the original is in the Egyptian Museum). The scenes showing the slaughter of animals on this wall were intended to provide the tomb owner with nourishment. He is also depicted here eating a meal. Two false doors in the west wall mark the place of offering. The procession of people bearing offerings, on the north wall, moves towards this point. Above the graceful female figures is the most famous scene of this tomb: Ti on a boat journey in a thicket of papyrus.

MEMPHIS

It is highly recommendable to combine a journey to Saqqâra with a visit to **Memphis ❹**, one-and-a-half kilometers farther south in a grove of palm trees near the village of Mîtrahîna. It was founded around 3000 BC by Menes, who was the legendary first king of the First Dynasty. Memphis's golden age was that of the Old Kingdom, despite the fact that it long afterwards was esteemed as the place where the kings were crowned. The strengthening of Christianity finally resulted in this heathen metropolis fading into complete obscurity. The founding of Fustât brought about the wholesale pillage of stones from the existing buildings of the city, which was not rediscovered until the 19th century.

To the right of the entrance of the **Open-air Museum** in the Memphis complex, protected by a concrete structure, lies the toppled ****Colossus of Ramses II**. This limestone statue, originally 13.5 meters in height (today only 10.5 meters), shows the Pharaoh dressed in royal clothing, with a pleated apron and the classical striped head covering, from the headband of which a massive stone uraeus rises whose "fiery breath shall destroy the enemies of the king."

The center of the complex is a beautiful ****Alabaster Sphinx**, which once guarded a temple dedicated to the god Ptah. The statue which measures 4.25 meters in length and eight meters in height, has no inscription whatsoever, but its style strongly suggests the Eighteenth Dynasty.

On the opposite side of the road you can see the walls of the **Embalming Site of Apis**, with its beautiful alabaster embalming tables dating from the Twenty-sixth Dynasty. This is where the sacred animal of Ptah, the Apis bull, was mummified before it was buried in the tombs of the necropolis of Memphis, in Saqqâra.

CAIRO (☎ 02)

ℹ️ The Ministry for Tourism is responsible for publishing a brochure called *Cairo by night and day*, in which you will find the most important addresses and very useful information. It is available in all of the big hotels or, alternatively, in branches of the **State Tourist Office**: Head office, 5 Sh. Adlî, tel. 3913454; also at the airport, tel. 667475; and at the pyramids, tel. 3850259. *Cairoscope* is a monthly calendar of events, with daily listings of culture and entertainment available throughout the city. Another useful source of information is a monthly magazine called *Egypt Today* which contains numerous useful addresses, a calendar of events and interesting informative articles.

🚖 *GETTING THERE:* Most visitors to Cairo arrive by plane. The international airport is situated at the northern edge of the city, in the suburb of Heliopolis. Before your departure from **Cairo International Airport** you should be aware that there are actually two (closely situated) airports: Terminal 1 – for all international flights, except those by Egypt Air; Terminal 2 – all Egypt Air flights.

🏨 Hotels are concentrated around the pyramids of Gîza (for those travelers seeking a little comfort and relaxation), in the city center (for those seeking excitement) and in Heliopolis (close to the airport for convenience, before continuing your journey).
🌟🌟🌟 **Helnan Shepherd**, Corniche an-Nîl, tel. 3553900, fax 3557284. **Cairo Marriott**, Gazîra Island, tel. 3408888, fax 3406667. **Le Meridien Le Caire**, Rôda Island, tel. 2905055, fax 2918591. **Nile Hilton**, Corniche an-Nîl, tel. 5780444, 5780666, fax 5780475. **Ramses Hilton**, Corniche an-Nîl, tel. 5754999, fax 5757152. **Semiramis**, Corniche an-Nîl, tel. 3557171, fax 3563020. **El-Gezîrah Sheraton**, Gazîra Island, tel. 3411555, fax 3405056. **Heliopolis Mövenpick**, Cairo International Airport Road, tel. 2470077, fax 4180761. **Swissotel El Salam**, Sh. 'Abd al-Hamîd Badâwî, tel. 2974000, fax 2976037. **Meridien Heliopolis**, Sh. 'Urûba, tel. 2905055, fax 2918591.
🌟🌟 **Arc en Ciel El-Borg**, Gazîra Island, tel. 3400978, fax 3403401. **El-Nil**, Garden City, tel. 3542800, fax 3552878. **President**, 22 Sh. Taha Husein, tel. 3400652, fax 3411752. **Victoria**, 66 Sh. al-Gumhûrîya, tel. 5892290, fax 5913008. **Windsor**, 19 Sh. al-Alfî, tel. 5921621.
🌟 **El Husein**, Md. Husein, near Khân al-Khalîlî, tel. 5918664, 5918089. **Green Valley**, 33 Sh. 'Abd al-Khâliq Sarwat, tel. 3936317. **New Hotel**, 21 Sh. Adlî, tel. 3927033, fax 3929555.
YOUTH HOSTELS: **El-Manial**, 135 Sh. 'Abd al 'Azîz as-Sa'ûd, tel. 840729.

Cairo

❌ In all of the luxury hotels you'll find at least one excellent restaurant serving both international and Egyptian specialties. As well as the luxury hotels, the following addresses are recommended:
ORIENTAL: **Abu Shakra**, 69 Sh. al-Qasr al-'Einî. **Arabesque**, 6 Sh. Qasr an-Nîl. **Felfela**, 15, Hôda Sha'arawî (side-street off Sh. Tal'at Harb); **Hagg Muhammad as-Samak**, Sh. 'Abd al-' Azîz (opposite the Omar Effendi department store). **Sofar**, Sh. Adlî. **Al-Hati**, Md. Halîm.
INTERNATIONAL: **Carroll**, 12 Sh. Qasr an-Nîl. **Estoril**, 12 Sh. Tal'at Harb, (entrance in the arcade off Sh. Qasr an-Nîl). **Paprika**, Corniche an-Nîl (beside the broadcasting building). **Rex**, Sh. 'Abd al-Khâliq Sarwat.
CAFÉS: **Groppi**, Md. Tal'at Harb. **Groppi's Garden**, Sh. 'Abd al-Khâliq Sarwat. **Indian Tea House**, Sh, Tal'at Harb (in the arcade). **Lappas**, Sh. Qasr an-Nîl.

🎷 *DISCOTHEQUES / NIGHTCLUBS* with live music and oriental shows featuring belly-dancing, dervish-dancing and oriental folklore are available in all luxury hotels. Otherwise, most nightclubs can be found along **Pyramids Road**. More tradition (and value for money) can be had in the **Granada** on Md. Opera, which features magicians as well as belly-dancing and oriental shows. The State Travel Agency – Misr Travel, offers a publication called *Cairo by night*. **Misr Travel**, 7 Sh. Tal'at Harb, tel. 3930010.

🏛 As a rule you should always be aware that one or another of the sights will be closed temporarily due to restoration. But Egypt is unique in that it is positively blessed with an unbelievable number of monuments, so you needn't be afraid of missing out on any sightseeing. *MUSEUMS:* **Egyptian Museum**, Md. at-Tahrîr, daily 9 am-5 pm, Fri 9-11:30 am and 1:30-5 pm. **Beit as Suheimî**, Darb al-Asfar, 9 am-4 pm. **Beshtak-Palast** (opposite the Barquq-Mosque), 9 am-4 pm. **Islamic Museum**, Md. Ahmad Mâhir, daily 9 am-5 pm, Fridays 9-11:15 am and 1:15-5 pm. **Coptic Museum**, old town, daily p am-5 pm. **Citadel**, daily 9 am-5 pm. *MOSQUES:* Unlike in other Islamic countries, almost all of the mosques in Egypt can be visited by non-Muslims, assuming suitable clothing is worn. Women will need a headscarf for the Al-Azhar Mosque. Before entering one must take off one's shoes, and sometimes fabric shoes are available to wear over your own (don't forget to tip for this!). On Fridays, from 11:30 am-1:30 pm, many of the mosques are closed to visitors.

➕ *HOSPITALS:* **Al-Salâm Hospital**, 3 Sh. Syria, Mohandisîn, tel. 3422780. **Al-Salâm International Hospital**, Corniche an-Nîl, Ma'âdî, tel. 3638050. **Anglo-American Hospital**, Al-Gazîra (next to the Cairo Tower), tel. 3406162. *24-HOUR PHARMACIES* are located in the center of the city: **Ataba-Pharmacy**, Md. al-'Ataba. **Esaaf Pharmacy**, 37 Sh. 26th July.

📱 *CITY TRANSPORTATION:* The red-and-white or blue **city buses** provide the main public transportation system in the inner city, but they are usually hopelessly overcrowded.
A good alternative is provided by the small, **white Mercedes buses,** which provide only seating spaces. From Md. 'Abd al-Mun'im Riyâd, for example, Bus Nr. 183 runs to the pyramids, Nr. 27 to the main train station and airport, Nr. 54 to the Citadel, Nr. 77 to the Khân al-Khalîlî.
Since 1987 the first **subway** in all of Africa has been in operation in Cairo. A red „M" in an octagonal star symbolizes the stations. City maps are displayed in all of the station entrances, and on these maps all the stops are clearly marked.

🚗 *DAY TRIPS:* **Organised city tours** and **trips** to the pyramids, Memphis and Saqqâra can be booked at any travel agent. Those travelers wishing to take their trips independently are best off taking taxis. Although the pyramiden of Gîza can be reached by public transportation without any problems (see above), Saqqâra and Memphis are situated outside the public transport route network.

GÎZA

🛏 ⊕⊕⊕ **Mena House Oberoi**, Pyramids Rd., tel. 3833222, fax 3837777. **Pyramids Park**, Alexandria Desert Rd., tel. 3838666, fax 3839000. **Jolie Ville Mövenpick**, Alexandria Desert Rd., tel. 3852555, fax 3835006. **Forte Grand Pyramids**, Alexandria Desert Rd., tel. 3830383, fax 3830023. **Oasis Hotel**, Alexandria Desert Rd., tel. 3831777, fax 3830916. **Sofitel Le Sphinx**, Alexandria Desert Rd., tel. 3837444, 3837555, fax 3834930. ⊕⊕ **Pyramids Hotel**, 198 Pyramids Rd., tel. 3835900, fax 3834974. ⊕ **Lido Hotel,** 465 Pyramids Rd., tel. 5730272, fax 5750292.

❌ *ORIENTAL:* **Christo's**, Pyramids Rd. (opposite the Mena House Oberoi), fish specialties. **Garden Felfela**, Cairo-Alex Desert Rd. **Sakkara Nest** and **El-Dâr**, both on the road to Saqqâra.

🏛 The number of tickets available for viewing the inside of the **Pyramid of Cheops** is restricted to 150 per day, even after the installation of an air-conditioning system. Tickets are sold at 9 am at a desk right by the pyramid. This rule will eventually also apply to the **Pyramid of Khafre**.

🚗 *DAY TRIPS:* A **desert ride** (for those with riding experience) from Gîza to Saqqâra will prove to be a memorable experience. Those shying away from the strain of the several-hour-long ride can settle for a shorter easier ride around the pyramids. Horses with guides can be hired at the caravanserai at the foot of the pyramids, opposite the Mena House Oberoi hotel.

CENTRAL EGYPT AND THE OASIS OF FAYYÛM

PYRAMIDS OF DAHSHÛR
OASIS OF FAYYÛM
ABYDOS AND DANDARA
THE WESTERN OASES

Central Egypt

THE *PYRAMIDS OF DAHSHÛR

The Nile Valley begins to the south of Cairo with fertile green fields and palm groves, the shining ribbon of the wide river and a beautiful network of irrigation canals. Whereas the desert often comes right up to the banks of the river on the eastern side, the fertile areas on the west bank get wider the farther upstream you go.

There are many places which can be reached in a day trip from Cairo which reflect the beauty of rural Egypt. Taking the road from Gîza going south, eight kilometers south of Saqqâra the *Pyramids of Dahshûr ❶ which date from the Ancient and Middle Egpytian Periods come into view. Because they adjoin a restricted military zone, they have only been accessible for the public since 1996. Directly at the entrance is the **Brick Pyramid of Sesostris III** which today is severely affected by weathering (originally it was 78 meters high, today it is only 27 meters). It dates from the end of the 12th Dynasty (1882–1842 BC). After another 2.5 kilometers the first real pyramid of Ancient Egypt can be seen: the so-called *Red Pyramid** (101 meters high) It was built by King Snefru, the first

ruler of the Fourth Dynasty and the father of Cheops, in around 2600 BC. The burial chamber can be visited, access to it is, however, rather difficult. The ruined **White Pyramid** of Amenemhet II follows (1933–1897 BC) and in the extreme south is the 97-meter-high *Bent Pyramid** of Snefru, which has two different angles of inclination, a characteristic of the last stage before the classical pyramid form was developed. In fact it was originally planned as the first "real" pyramid, not – as in the case of its predecessors – as a stepped construction. However damage to the building work apparently required a correction to the angle of inclination and reinforcement of the foundations.

Beside this is the 30-meter-high **Black Brick Pyramid**, built by Amenemhet III (1843–1794 BC) who, probably because of statistical problems with this particular pyramid, had a second one built at the edge of the oasis of Fayyûm.

Continuing along the main road again, it is another 50 kilometers to Gerza (Arabic: *Jirza*) and to the turn-off for the *Pyramid of Maidûm ❷, the step tower of which can be seen from a great distance on a clear day, in shimmering white on the horizon. It is in many respects an oddity, above all because it actually consists of three polished limestone-covered

Left: Water is life.

CENTRAL EGYPT

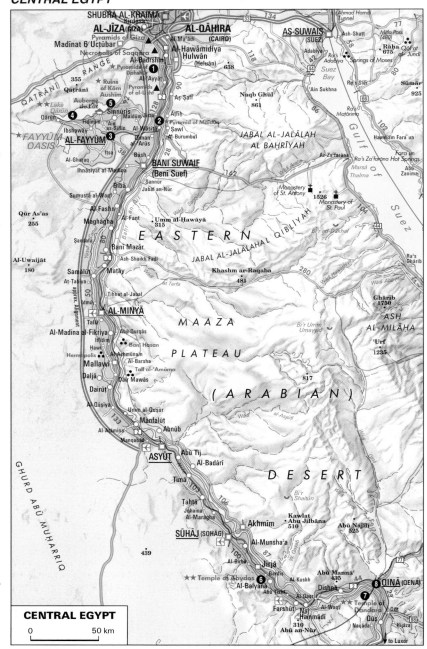

SHUBRĀ AL-KHAIMA
Kirdāsa
AL-JĪZA (GIZA)   AL-QĀHIRA (CAIRO)
Pyramids of Giza
Madīnat 6 Uctūbar   AL-Ma'ādi
Al-Hawāmidīya
Necropolis of Saqqāra   Hulwān (Heluān)
Al-Badrshin
Pyramids of   Al-Ayyāt ①
Dahshūr
Ruins of Kōm   Pyramids of al-Lisht
355   Qaṭrānī   Aushim
315
Auberge   Maidūm-Jīza
du Lac   Sinnūris   Al-Wāsiṭa
Lake   ④   ⑤   Saww
Qārūn   Fīdimim   'Umm   Pyramid of Maidūm ②
Qārūn   Ain   al-'Arūs
Ibshewāy   as-Sīlīn ③   'Umm al-Burumbul
FAYYŪM   AL-FAYYŪM   al-'Arūs
OASIS   Itsa   Būsh
Al-Gharaq   BANĪ SUWAIF (Benī Suef)
Ihnāsiyat al-Madīna
Bibā
Sumustá al-Wāqī   Jabal an-Nūr
Sannūr
Qūr Aṣ'as   Al-Fashn
255   Maghāgha   Al-Fant
Sandafa   Umm al-Hawāyā
Banī Mazār
Al-Uwaijāt   Ash-Shaikh Fadl
180   Samālūṭ
At-Tabiya   Matāy
Tihnat al-Jabal   At Tarfa   Khashm ar-Raqaba
Idmū   481
approx. Alignment
AL-MINYĀ
Ṭalla
Al-Madīna al-Fikrīya   Abū Qurqās
Iṭfīḥ   Banī Hasan
Hawt
Hermopolis   Al-Ashmūnain
Mallawī   Tall al-'Amārna
Al-Barsha
Daljā   Dair Mawās
Dairūṭ
Al-Qūsīya   Umm al-Qusūr
Manfalūṭ
Al-Atāmina   Abnūb
Manqabad
ASYŪṬ   Abū Tīj
Al-Badārī
Tīma
Tahtā
Johaina
Al-Marāgha
SŪHĀJ (SOHAG)   Akhmim
439   Al-Munsha'a
Al-Birba   Jirjā
Bardis
★★ Temple of Abydos   Al-Kushh
Al-Balyanā   Abū Manna'
Abū Tisht   Disha'
Al-Qasr
Farshūṭ   Al-Waqf
Naj' Hammādi   ★ Temple of Dandara
Abū an-Nūr   Qūṣ
310   Naqāda
Hijāza
to Luxor

SHUBRĀ AL-KHAIMA
134
33
AS-SUWAIS (SUEZ)
Ahmad Hamdi Tunnel
77
Ash-Shaṭṭ   Mitla Pass (480)
Adābiya   Rāha 675   Qaḷ'at al-Jundī
Ra's Adabīya   Springs of Moses
638   Suez Bay
Naqb Ghūl   'Ain Sukhna   Ra's Sūr
861   Ra's Matārinīya
JABAL AL-JALĀLAH   Hammām Farā'un
AL BAHRĪYAH   Az-Za'farāna   Fara'un
Marsā   Ra's Za'farāna Hot Springs
Thalma   Abū Zanima
Monastery of St. Antony
1526   Monastery of St. Paul
162   Bi'r as'ad Dākhal
JABAL AL-JALĀLAHAL QIBLĪYAH   Ra's Ghārib
Khashm ar-Raqaba
481   Wādī Hawāshīya   Wādī Abū Had
Ghārib 1750
Bi'r Umm Umayyid   ASH AL-MILĀHA
MAAZA   'Urf 1235
PLATEAU
817
(ARABIAN)   Wādī al-Asyūṭī
DESERT
Bi'r Shaitūn
Kawlat Abū Jilbāna   Abū Najli 525
510
435   77
Dandara   QINĀ (QENA) ⑧
⑦

CENTRAL EGYPT

0   50 km

36

pyramids. The innermost pyramid was a seven-stepped, 72-meter-high construction. This was covered, soon after it had been completed, by a second mantle, with eight steps, which was higher and wider than the first by 10 meters. But then the architects of King Snefru, who also built two more huge pyramids in Dahshûr, discovered the "pure form" and so they turned the stepped pyramid of Maidûm into a true pyramid, which rose over a square ground plan, with a side length of 144.3 meters, to a height of 92 meters. Today, as a result of the effects of the elements and thousands of years of plundering, it almost looks like a Babylonian ziggurat or temple tower. A 25-meter-high cone of debris surrounds the lower third of the true pyramid, above which only the third to the seventh steps can still be seen today.

THE *OASIS OF FAYYÛM

To the south of Maidûm, near Beni Suef, is the beginning of one of the main roads to the *Oasis of Fayyûm in the Province of Fayyûm, which can also be reached on a desert road from Gîza. The 1,800 square kilometer oasis lies in a depression of the Sahara. This depression is irrigated not by artesian wells, but by the Bahr Yûsuf, the River of Joseph. The annual floods once reached Fayyûm along this tributary of the Nile, which branches off north of Asyût (nowadays from the Ibrahîmîya Canal), and, during a long geological process, the whole area gradually turned into a swampy lake district. But of the ancient Egyptian *Pa-Yôm*, the sea which gave Fayyûm its name, only Lake Qârûn, now reduced to a sixth of its original size, remains.

Little has been preserved of all these ancient places, yet the journey through Fayyûm is charming, if for nothing else then for its scenery. This intensively farmed land is known as the garden of Cairo, providing the entire city with grain, fruit, vegetables and flowers. Now and again you can still see the typical dove towers of Fayyûm on the edges of the picturesque villages. These villages, with their houses built so closely to one another, sometimes almost seem to resemble medieval castles rising from the green plain.

In the heart of the oasis is the provincial capital, **Madînat al-Fayyûm** ❸ which, despite its population of 300,000, possesses little of the atmosphere which would be typical of a large city. The main attractions in the town center are four loud, creaking *water wheels which, with huge paddles, transport the waters of the Bahr Yûsuf into tanks – nowadays only for museum purposes.

A popular place for day trips in the northwest of Fayyûm is **Lake Qârûn** ❹, 50 kilometers long and 12 kilometers wide. It is salty and rich in fish. The country road leads through the towns of 'Ain as-Sillîn, with a small freshwater spring in the middle of a beautiful park, and **Fidîmîn** and through the fruit plantations of Fayyûm straight to the beautifully renovated Hotel **Auberge du Lac** at the lake.

To the east of the lake on the desert road to Cairo are the ruins of *Kôm Aushîm ❺ (Arabic: *Kawm Awshîm*), the ancient *Karanis*. Two small temples and several mud brick buildings of the Ptolomaic city, some still partly painted, have been well preserved. One of the more interesting finds made at Karanis was a number of papyri which tell us a lot about the life of the Greek settlers.

**TEMPLE OF ABYDOS

One of the great sights of Central Egypt is the **Temple of Abydos** ❻ which was constructed by **Seti I** (1290–1279 BC). Generally it can best be visited via Luxor, which lies around 180 kilometers to the south. Once linked to the Nile by a canal, the unusually laid-out

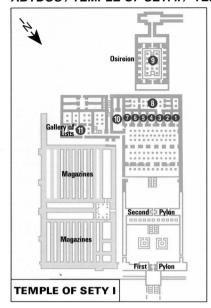

TEMPLE OF SETY I

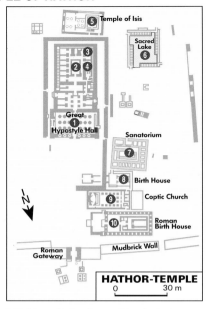

HATHOR-TEMPLE
0   30 m

complex rises in two terraces, both with open courtyards, to a covered temple building. Here, seven parallel processional paths cut through hypostyle halls and eventually lead to seven sanctuaries. Ramses II completed the temple after his father's death. He had all seven of the planned entrances, with the exception of the central portal, walled up and decorated with inscriptions and large reliefs.

The murals of the first **hypostyle hall**, with 24 papyrus-sheaf columns, also come from the time of Ramses II, as even those unschooled in ancient Egyptian history can probably tell. For, in contrast to the delicately raised bas-relief favored by Seti I, Ramses preferred sunken reliefs carved into the surface. The partially-colored relief cycles of the seven **Sanctuaries** are especially interesting. These were dedicated to the gods **Horus ❶**, **Isis ❷**, **Osiris ❸**, **Amen-Ra ❹**, **Ra-Harakhti ❺** and **Ptah ❻**, and to **Seti**

Right: Skilfully raised relief of Ramses II in the Temple of Abydos.

I ❼ himself. In almost identical pictures they show the king opening the shrine in the morning, offering incense to the cultic image and then anointing it (with his little finger) and bringing it jewelry and strips of cloth as garments. At the back of the room he is usually seen making his offerings in front of the god's barque. In reality, this would have stood in front of the shrine.

From the Osiris Sanctuary you enter the diagonal **Osiris Hall ❽**, a beautiful shrine with reliefs and three cult chapels. Directly behind this, outside the temple, is the cenotaph of the king, the so-called **Osireion ❾**: a monumental subterranean hall of pillars, which is entered via a 110-meter-long tunnel and several chambers. Above this was once probably a tree-covered hill, a symbol of the primeval hill of the beginning of the universe. Today you can only see the 10 monolithic granite pillars which are half sunken below the rising ground water level.

The Osireion is reached through the side wings where, next to the lovely

Chambers of Worship of Ptah ⑩, the famous **Gallery of Lists** ⑪ is found. Crown Prince Ramses stands with his father Seti I in front of a list with oval rings of names, covering the entire wall, which names all Seti I's ancestors starting with Menes, the founder of the empire. Illegitimate rulers, like the Hyksos or Amarna kings, were omitted, for they did not rule according to the official royal dogma.

****TEMPLE OF DANDARA**

Between Abydos and Luxor, near the provincial capital Qena, lies the ****Temple of Dandara** ⑦, the center of worship of **Hathor**, the goddess of love and music and the great mother and goddess of the sky. Once the center of a capital of the sixth Upper Egyptian province, the temple complex enclosed by a huge mud brick wall now lies in solitude on the edge of the desert. The history of the shrine can be traced back to Cheops, but those parts which have been preserved were not built until Ptolemaic-Roman times.

In the center is the temple building of Hathor. The pylon was never finished, so as soon as you walk through the Roman gateway you find yourself in front of the **Great Hypostyle Hall** ①, whose massive capitals dominate the façade, along with the face of the goddess whose ears are those of a cow. Twenty-four monumental columns support the ceiling of the hall, representing the sky, and is decorated with astronomical pictures, winged suns and flying vultures. The central procession path rises in classical Ptolemaic style through another smaller hall with columns and two anterooms for the sacrificial altars and shrines of the guest gods. You then come to the **Holy of Holies** ②, which is enclosed protectively by a circle of 11 chambers. The mural paintings, some of which were hacked away during the Christian era, show scenes of sacrifice and worship which the king, who is often not even named, is performing before Hathor and her god-husband Horus of Edfu. The most beautiful reliefs can be seen in the **crypts**, a secret system of pas-

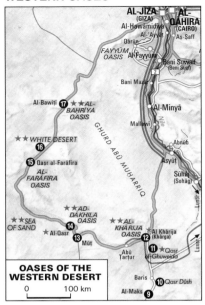

OASES OF THE WESTERN DESERT

0   100 km

is a large city, but for travelers is merely a stage on the way to Luxor, 62 kilometers away or to the Red Sea Coast.

THE WESTERN OASES

While Asyût was once an important starting point for a trip to the oases of the Western Desert, the road connection to Luxor now offers the attractive possibility of combining the classic destinations Luxor and Aswân with an oasis trip, without having to make any detours. According to the time available, and the degree of interest, it is best to plan a trip of several days, starting in Luxor, or to integrate it into the 1300-kilometer-long trip from Luxor to Cairo (or in the other direction).

The **new oasis route**, approximately 270 kilometers in length, branches off from the road along the east bank to Esna, about 15 kilometers south of the Nile bridge near Luxor and after a drive of about three hours through stony desert, you come to an escarpment, from which you have a grandiose panorama over the huge oasis depression of ****Khârga**. This is the "outermost" (Arabic: *al-khârija*) in the chain of the four oases which continues northwards with Dâkhla (Arabic: *ad-dâkhila* "the innermost"), Farâfra and Al-Bahrîya. The opening of the underground fresh-water reservoir is intended to turn the oasis belt into a second Nile Valley. However, the expectations which were raised by the project, which was begun in 1960, have only been partly fulfilled, as agriculture here has been confronted with several unexpected results, such as salination of the topsoil, a lowering of the water pressure because of the overloading of the artesian wells, or the fact that despite significant incentives, Nile Valley farmers have shown little interest in resettling the area. The second large step for the *New Valley*, as the southwest border province of Egypt is named, followed with the construction of the long-planned *Toshka Canal*. A concrete

sageways where the cultic images depicted on the walls were kept. Through the entrance from the inner anteroom ➌ you come to the **New Year's Chapel** ➍, with an interesting ceiling relief of the goddess Nut, in which the first rays of the morning sun are shown shining down onto the Hathor Temple.

The temple roof offers a fine view of the whole temple area: to the south a small **Temple of Isis** ➎ from the time of Augustus and the **Holy Lake** ➏, picturesquely surrounded by palm trees; north of the temple building the mud brick remains of the **Sanatorium** ➐, a sort of temple clinic, two so-called **Mammisi** ➑ and ➓, which are chapels in honour of the divine birth of the king, and the ruins of a **Coptic basilica** ➒ dating from the fifth century AD.

Three kilometers east of Dandara the last bridge before Luxor crosses the Nile and leads to the provincial capital of **Qena** ➑, which with 250,000 inhabitants

Right: The Temple of Hathor in Dandara.

Central Egypt

canal, 800 kilometers in length, is to bring water from the large reservoir to Farâfra, with the aim of increasing the percentage of agricultural land in the region from 5 percent to 25 percent of the total surface area.

The southernmost town of the oasis Khârga is **Al-Maks** ❾. It is situated on an ancient caravan route, the *Darb al-'arba'în*, the "40 day track", to the Sudan. Even in antiquity this route was of great importance and was protected by a series of fortresses, the southernmost of which was the **Qasr Dûsh** ❿, which contains the ruins of a Roman temple to Isis . Several kilometers south of Khârga town, the administrative center of the New Valley province, is the ★**Qasr al-Ghuwaida** ⓫, which has a well-preserved Amen temple dating from Persian times.

In the town of ★**Khârga** ⓬ the little crooked old lanes of the bazaar are ideal for strolling and shopping and the **Archeological Museum**, which opened in 1988, documents the rich history of the oases right back to the Paleolithic Age.

Outside the gates of the town in the middle of a palm grove is the ★**Temple of Amen**, dedicated to him in about 500 BC by the Persian King Darius I. Next to it stretch the ruins of the Roman city of ★**Hibis**, with impressive mud brick buildings of the early Christian ★★**Cemetery of Bagawât**.

The 200-kilometer-long stretch of road between Khârga and **Mût** ⓭, the main town of ★★**Dâkhla**, leads through a desert area rich in variety. With 80,000 inhabitants, the so-called "inner oasis" is not only the largest, but also the most beautiful of all the oases of the New Valley. The shimmering pink-colored rocks of the escarpment, which can always be seen on the horizon, gave rise to its poetic name: "The Pink Oasis." Palm groves and orchards complete the idyllic scenery. On the northern outskirts of Mût a sign points the way to the **Mût Tourism Wells**, a hot spring, typical of the whole oasis chain. This spring has been channeled into thermal baths, and in contrast to some of the more romantic places, is easily accessi-

ble. Surely the most picturesque place in all of Dâkhla is ★**Al-Qasr** ⑭. Sadly, its beautifully medieval town center was, in part, very badly damaged recently as the result of extremely heavy rainfall. A few kilometers outside Al-Qasr are the Roman ★**Tombs of Al-Muzawwaka**, with colorful paintings of ancient Egyptian scenes of the cult of the dead. A little farther to the southwest you come to the Roman **Temple of Amen at Dair al-Hajar**, which is still half-buried under the desert sand.

An asphalt road now joins Dâkhla with the two northern oases of the New Valley. This road arches into the Libyan Desert, just touching the edge of the ★★**Great Sea of Sand**, with its huge waves of dunes about 100 kilometers west of **Al-Mawhûb**. About 130 kilometers farther on you come to **Qasr al-Farâfra** ⑮, the pretty main town of the oasis **Farâfra**. To the north of here the ★★**White Desert**

⑯ stretches to the edge of the high escarpment. The landscape of the White Desert was formed by erosion, and has bizarre limestone formations which rise from the flats like strange and wonderful animals.

At ★★**Al-Bahrîya**, the "northern" oasis, you will find splendid lush oasis gardens surrounding the main town, **Bawîtî** ⑰. At the foot of the cliffs of Bawîtî and its sister town **Al-Qasr**, is an ocean of fruit trees and date palms, on the edges of which are several hot springs. The oasis gained unexpected world-wide fame in the summer of 1999 with the discovery of burial fields with (so far) 105 mummies, some of which have valuable ornamentation. The *Valley of the Golden Mummies*, where it is supposed there are up to 10,000 mummies is not yet open to visitors. Since November 1999 however, the ★**Temple of Alexander the Great** in Al-Qasr and some tombs in the region around Bawîtî have been opened. The ★**Tomb of Banentiu** (26th Dynasty), in particular, has beautiful paintings.

Above: Palms flourish in the western desert thanks to the "New Valley" irrigation project.

Central Egypt

FAYYÛM AND THE OASES

🚓 *SECURITY:* The Nile valley between Cairo and Luxor is still officially considered unsafe. You can still travel to the area, but freedom of movement for tourists is certainly limited: police escorts accompany foreign travelers along the auto routes toward the south; the number of trains licensed to carry foreigners has been reduced; in Fayyûm you must be prepared to experience route and area restrictions (for foreigners only!). At worst, you'll be sent away by one of the omnipresent security guards. A good point is that for drives through the oases there are no restrictive conditions, but only if you avoid Asyût. **Tip:** Always take your passport with you, even on day trips.

🚌 *GETTING THERE:* **Scheduled flights** by *Egypt Air* depart Cairo twice weekly, via Dâkhla and on to Khârga.
Buses, operated by the *Upper Egypt Bus Company,* depart Cairo several times a day heading towards Fayyûm. (Departure in Cairo: bus station for the time being is at Md. Turgumân, a few intersections west of the main train station, or else at Md. Ahmad Hilmî at the main train station). Buses from the same company drive daily into the oases of Al-Bahrîya, Farâfra, Dâkhla and Khârga. Departure in Cairo from the bus station Md. Salâh ad-Din below the citadel; minibuses depart from Ibn-Tulûn Mosque. There is also a once-daily bus connection between Khârga and Luxor.
Group taxis to Madînat al-Fayyûm depart from Mîdân Gîza, near Cairo University.
Those wishing to visit Fayyûm or the oases of the New Valley with their own car or a rental **car**, should enquire in advance about possible restricted zones or necessary advance authorization! Information is also available from the **Automobile Club of Egypt**, Cairo, 10 Sh. Qasr an-Nîl, tel. 5743355.

FAYYÛM OASIS(☎ 084)

ℹ️ **Tourist Information**, Governorate Building, Madînat al-Fayyûm, tel. 322586.
🏨 😊😊😊 **Auberge du Lac**, Lake Qârûn, tel. 700002. fax 700730. **New Panorama Village**, Shakshûk, Lake Qârûn, tel. 701314, fax 701757.
😊😊 **Queen**, Madînat al-Fayyûm, 4 Sh. Minshat. tel. 326819.
😊 **Ein el-Sellin**, 'Ain as-Sillîn (nahe Sanhûr), tel. 327471. **Oasis Tourist Village**, Shakshûk, Lake Qârûn, tel. 701565.
YOUTH HOSTELS: **Youth Hostel**, Madînat al-Fayyûm, Al-Hadîqa Nr. 7, tel. 323682.
❌ The fish restaurants around Qârûn Lake are a popular destination for people from Cairo and are usually overcrowded on Fridays. The **Auberge Fayoum Oberoi** in the Auberge du Lac lake hotel is very elegant. The restaurants in the **New Panorama Village** and **Oasis Tourist Village** hotels are also highly recommended. Good seafood can be had in the **Caféteria Gebel az-Zêna**, a few kilometers west of the Auberge du Lac hotel.

THE WESTERN OASES

AL-BAHRÎYA (☎ 018)

ℹ️ **Tourist Information Al-Bahrîya**, Bawîtî, City Council (beside the post office), tel. 802222.
🏨 😊😊 **Ahmed's Safari Camp**, outside Bawîtî on the road to Sîwa, tel. 802090. **International Health Center**, Bawîtî, tel. 802322. **New Oasis**, Bawîtî, tel. 803030. 😊 **Alpenblick**, Bawîtî, tel. 802184. **El-Beshmo Lodge**, Bawîtî, tel. 802177. **Resthouse Al-Menagem**, Al-Menagem-Mine, 42 km northeast of Bawîtî in the direction of Cairo.
🚓 *DAY TRIPS:* **Off-road tours** to the White Desert and hot springs can be organized in Bawîtî.

DÂKHLA (☎ 092)

🏨 😊😊 **Mebarez**, Mût, on the road to Farâfra, tel. 821524. 😊 **Anwar**, in the center of Mût, tel. 821566. **Bedouin Camp**, Ad-Duhûs, north of Mût, tel. 8250605. **Dar al-Wafdên**, Mût, tel. 941503. **Gardens Hotel**, Mût, tel. 821577. **Mut Bungalows**, Mût, tel. 941503. **Tourism Wells Resthouse**, on the western edge of Mût. **Government Tourist Chalets**, by the hot springs of Mût and Al-Qasr (advance booking through the Tourist Information Office in Khârga.)

FARÂFRA (☎ 046)

🏨 😊😊 **Badit El Farafra Village & Hotel**, Qasr al-Farafra, reservations can be made at the office in Cairo, tel. (02) 3458524. **New Resthouse**, Qasr al-Farâfra (at the bus station).
🚓 *DAY TRIPS:* In Qasr al-Farâfra **off-road tours** into the White Desert are available.

KHÂRGA (☎ 092)

ℹ️ **New Valley Tourist Information**, opposite the Oasis Hotel, provides information on all of the oases, tel. 901205.
🏨 😊😊😊 **The Pioneers Hotel**, Khârga (on exiting the town towards Asyût), tel. 4306820. 😊😊 **El-Kharga Oasis**, Khârga, tel. 901500. 😊 **El-Wâdî el-Gedîd Tourist Chalets**, Khârga, (beside the State Tourist Officen), tel. 900728. **Hamadalla**, Khârga, tel. 900638, fax 905017. **Resthouse Al-Nasr Tourism Wells**, 17 km south of Khârga. **Bulaq Resthouse**, Bulaq, 30 km south of Khârga. **Resthouse Baris**, Bârîs, 80 km south of Khârga.

THEBES: CITY OF A HUNDRED GATES

LUXOR
KARNAK
THEBES WEST

**LUXOR

Luxor, a small town with around 40,000 inhabitants is situated about seven hundred kilometers south of Cairo in the province of Qena. With its elegant luxury hotels and its international airport, it is a fully developed center of tourism for those interested in Ancient Egypt.

Traces of settlements from the distant past have been found. Yet it was the Theban Prince Mentuhotep II, who united the land of the Nile after the horrors of the First Intermediate Period and who established Thebes' fame. In about 2037 BC, it became the capital of the empire for the first time. But this was just an episode, for the kings of the Twelfth Dynasty moved back to the strategically more important north. Thebes' finest hour came at the onset of the Eighteenth Dynasty, half a millenium later, when its rise to becoming the shining center of the Egyptian Empire began. Once again Theban princes fought for the unity of the land, this time against the Hyksos, the Asiatic foreign rulers who had settled in the Nile Delta. For a period of 200 years Thebes retained its status as the capital – until King Amenhotep IV, the first great prophet of monotheism who is better

Left: In the Great Hypostyle Hall of Karnak.

known to history under the name Akhnaton, left the residence of his ancestors and moved his court to Amarna. His descendants ultimately returned to the north, but Thebes remained the religious center of the country. Indeed, the temple of Amen-Ra in Karnak became the heart of a kingdom of god on earth, and played a significant political role until the town was destroyed by the Assyrians in the seventh century BC. The holy city never recovered from this blow, even though new buildings were constructed under the Ptolemies and the Romans.

**The Temple of Luxor

Only a few paces away from the Winter Palace Hotel, you will find one of the best-preserved temple complexes in Egypt towering up on the bank of the Nile. This is the **Temple of Luxor ❶**, dedicated to the Theban trinity of gods, Amen, Mut and Khonsu. An inscription tells how King Amenhotep III had the holy shrine built of "fine sandstone," with "a bed of frankincense on a floor of silver," and with a wide courtyard "the columns of which are lotus buds." But this only refers to the temple tract at the back with the various chambers of worship, the great columned court and the monumental colonnade.

The temple was completed in its present form only 100 years afterwards, when Ramses II had another columned courtyard and a huge pylon built in front of the colonnade.

A visit to the temple starts at these gate towers. You will find the best view from the **Sphinx Avenue ❶**, which leads to the temple from the north. It is the last part of a three-kilometer processional path which led to the temple city of Amen in Karnak. Hundreds of sphinxes, between which flowers and trees were planted, once lined the magnificent avenue, which has still only been partly excavated. In the New Kingdom it consisted of ram sphinxes, but during restorations which were carried out under Nektanebo I (Thirtieth Dynasty) these were replaced by the classical type of sphinx, with the head of a king.

The reliefs of the great **Pylon of Ramses II ❷** (24 meters high, 65 meters total width) are best seen – and photographed! – in the early morning light. The reliefs and texts portray the Battle of Kadesh, which Ramses II glorified in all his temple buildings as a victory over the Hittites.

Four baboons decorate the pedestals of the 25-meter-high pink granite **obelisk ❸** in front of the east tower. Only the pedestal remains of its counterpart which would normally face it; Muhammad 'Alî presented it as a gift to France. Since 1836 it has stood on the Place de la Concorde in Paris.

Of the six **Colossi of Ramses II ❹** which once stood in front of the pylon, only the two seated figures of grey granite (15.6 meters high) and a considerably restored statue (right) have been preserved.

The adjacent **Columned Court of Ramses II ❺** (50 x 57 meters) is enclosed by a double row of 74 smooth columns with closed papyrus capitals. The same type of column can be seen in front of the **Granite Chapel of Queen Hatshepsut ❻**.

The **Mosque of Abû al-Haggâg ❼** in the northeast corner of the courtyard is impressive not only because of its beautiful walls, but also because of the lofty heights to which it rises. This shows how deeply the temple was once buried under the sand.

A relief on the south wall ❽ of the adjacent Columned Court of Ramses II shows how the pylon must have looked in ancient times. It depicts a festive procession, marking the dedication ceremonies, led by 17 princes who are proceeding towards the pylon, with its two obelisks, the six colossi and four poles with flags flying.

The **Temple of Amenhotep III** starts with the **Colonnade ❾** (52 x 20 meters),

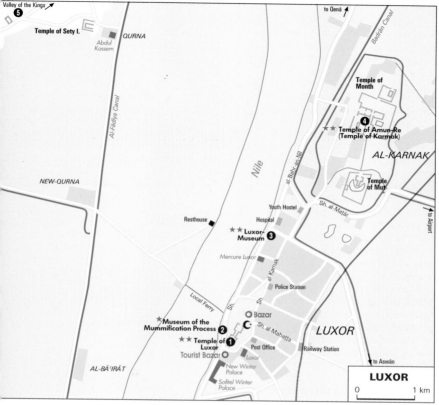

of which the 14 papyrus columns with open capitals are almost 16 meters high. The fine reliefs on the side walls (from the time of Tutankhamen and Horemheb) show the *Opet Festival*, the greatest state festival of the New Kingdom: Amen and his wife Mut and their son Khonsu visited Amen's "Southern Sanctuary" in Luxor every year at the time of the flooding of the Nile. The statues of the gods traveled the short journey from Karnak to Luxor in a magnificent ship which was towed upstream along the banks of the Nile. A colorful crowd, soldiers, musicians and dancers accompanied the procession, at the end of which sacrificial rites took place. (The journey there is shown on the right, the return journey on the left).

A further **Hypostyle Court** ⑩ (52 x 46 meters) opens out behind the colonnade. This is surrounded by a double row of ribbed papyrus-bundle columns. Pictures of this court of the Temple of Luxor were sent around the world in 1989; during work on the foundations Egyptian archeologists made a sensational find: an ancient store of more than 20 statues, most of which were in excellent condition. The statues of gods and kings are all in stone; the oldest date from the time of Tuthmosis III (Luxor Museum).

The covered temple building begins on the south face of the courtyard with a small hall of 32 columns, which is like a stone thicket of papyrus. The adjoining room was also once a hypostyle hall, but

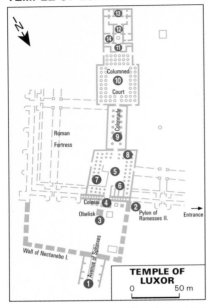

TEMPLE OF LUXOR

0   50 m

pictures on a relief cycle portraying the legend of the birth of the Egyptian king, in this case Amenhotep III. The most interesting scene is in the central section on the long wall: the ibis-headed god Thot, a messenger of Amen-Ra, tells the Queen Mother that she is to bear a holy child.

On the Nile Promenade, diagonally opposite the Luxor Temple the **★Museum of the Mummification Process ❷** shows animal mummies, coffins, implements used in mummification, and much more, illustrating this aspect of the ancient Egyptians' provision for life after death.

★★KARNAK

Three kilometers from the Temple of Luxor, near the village of **★★Karnak**, which has joined into one settlement with Luxor, is Egypt's largest holy place, the temple city of the King of the Gods Amen-Ra. The way there leads along the new, spacious Nile Promenade. On foot it takes a good half hour. A ride in a horse-drawn carriage is perhaps a more inviting alternative, especially on hot days.

After a short distance, the modern edifice of the **★★Luxor Museum ❸** can be seen on the Corniche to the right. The museum, which opened in 1976, offers an outstanding view into the art and history of old Thebes. The items on exibit are clearly displayed, well illuminated and have explanations in several languages.

About one kilometer farther on, the street branches off to the **★★Temple of Karnak ❹**. Once the religious center of an empire, Karnak is today a gigantic archeological site with an overwhelming number of individual buildings. For 2000 years – from the period of the Middle Kingdom to Ptolemaic times – all the great Pharaohs of Egyptian history built temples, chapels and monuments here, and undertook restorations, extensions and conversions.

In front of the temple you first cross a small, almost inconspicuous wooden

was rebuilt by Roman soldiers in the third century BC as a **chapel ⓫** for the worship of their emperor. They covered the old reliefs with a layer of plaster and painted over them.

The complex of the cult chambers begins with the **Hall of Four Pillars**, where the sacrificial altar once stood, followed directly by the **Sanctuary ⓬** for the divine barque. The large granite shrine was donated by Alexander the Great and shows the conqueror, dressed as a Pharaoh, performing sacrifices to the gods. Behind it is another ritual chamber and the **Chamber for the Cult Statue ⓭**. In front of the barque sanctuary a door to the left leads to one of the most famous rooms of the temple. Unfortunately, the reliefs of the **Birth Room ⓮** have not been well preserved, due to the iconoclastic destruction carried out by Akhnaton. With the help of the morning sun (or a flashlight) you can make out some of the

Right: Pharaoh's enigmatic smile (statue of Ramses II in the Temple of Luxor).

bridge. The ditch beneath it was once part of a harbor basin into which a branch canal flowed from the Nile. Heavily-laden barges traveled along this canal to the temple, carrying the most varied assortment of wares and building materials, which were always in demand.

This is where Amen-Ra's magnificent river barge headed when it set off on festival processions to Luxor or the western necropolis. Two **Obelisks of Seti II** once ornamented the well-preserved **wharves**; today only one of them is still standing. An avenue of 40 **ram-headed sphinxes** leads from here directly to the temple. The sacred animals of Amen are set on high pedestals, and on each of these, protected by their heads, is a small statue of Ramses II (1279 –13 BC).

The eight-meter-thick surrounding wall is built of bricks of Nile mud. Integrated within it, the largest gate of Pharaonic Egypt forms the entrance to the temple city of Amen-Ra. This **First Pylon** ❶ (113 x 43.5 x 15 meters) was never completed. The blocks remained unpolished and have neither reliefs nor inscriptions on them. An exact dating of the building has only been possible since 1985, when at the back of the southern pylon, the remains of a **brick ramp** ❷ were found, containing bricks stamped with the name of Nektanebo I (380–62 BC). This ramp is evidence of the building methods of the ancient Egyptians, who used this kind of brick scaffolding.

The **Great Court** has a surface area of 8,000 square meters, making it the largest temple court in the country. Dominating the court is a 21-meter-high column, the only one of 10 papyrus bundle columns of the **Kiosk of Taharqa** ❸ that has remained standing. Stone barriers once connected the individual columns with one another, which were once roofed-in by light wood or other material.

When Amen-Ra embarked on a procession there were many ceremonial stops made along the way. Two of the shrine stages, which only came alive on feast days, are found in the area of the Great Court: the **Chapel of Seti II** ❹ and

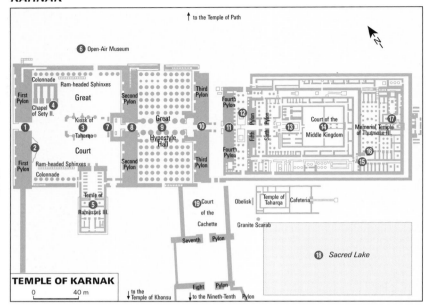

TEMPLE OF KARNAK

0   40 m

the **Temple of Ramses III** ❺ (1191–89 BC) which in exemplary fashion unites all the typical elements of an Egyptian temple.

To the north of the great court is the **Open-air Museum** ❻. There you can see fragments of the oldest shrines in Karnak. The undisputed showpiece here is the **White Chapel** which was built by Sesostris I for the celebrations marking the 30th jubilee of his reign. The charming building with 16 pillars of white limestone is the oldest chapel in Karnak. Its wonderfully detailed reliefs show the king making offerings to the god Amen-Min, a syncretistic fusion of Amen with Min, the god of fertility. Its fine reliefs make the **Alabaster Chapel of Amenhotep I** opposite well worth a visit. They also show the king making offerings to Amen-Min.

On returning to the Great Court, turn to face the Second Pylon of Horemheb. Two

Right: Ram-headed sphinxes in the Great Court of the Temple of Karnak.

pink granite **Colossi of Ramses II** ❼ flank the entrance of the dilapidated gateway structure. The left one is a statue of the king 15 meters high, with a smaller statue of his daughter and wife Merit-Amen. It was usurped during the Twenty-first Dynasty by Pinedjem (c. 1065–45 BC), one of the priest-kings of the Theban Theocracy.

Passing through a small anteroom and the 29.5-meter-high portal of the very dilapidated **Second Pylon of Horemheb** ❽ you come to the architectural masterpiece of Karnak: the **Great Hypostyle Hall** ❾. One hundred and thirty-four papyrus bundle columns rise like a monumental petrified forest covering an area of 5,406 square meters. The columns of the central nave are 24 meters high and have a circumference of 10 meters, which increases to an amazing 15 meters at their open flower capitals. The 122 columns of the side aisles have a circumference of "only" 6.4 meters and are 14 meters high. Originally the whole hall was roofed over. The difference in height from the

Luxor

central nave to the side aisles was bridged by huge trellised windows (some are very well preserved). Light fell through them onto the processional path of the divine barque, yet the side aisles were always in semi-darkness. For over half a century the Great Hypostyle Hall was under construction: Amenhotep III built the 12-columned central colonnade; the Second Pylon of Horemheb formed the foundations of the side aisles; Seti I and his son Ramses II decorated the Great Hypostyle Hall with scenes of sacrificial rites and processions: the father in delicate high relief (left), the son in a sunk relief (right).

At the back of the badly destroyed **Third Pylon of Amenhotep III** ❿ the more than 30-meter-long Nile ship of Amen-Ra, in which the King of the Gods sailed on the Nile to his festival processions is depicted. Of the original four obelisks which once stood in front of the **Fourth Pylon of Tuthmosis I** ⓫, only one still exists; a monolith of pink granite, 23 meters high and weighing 143 tons, with a dedication of the same

Tuthmosis I who also built the **Fifth Pylon**. In front of the Fifth Pylon Hatshepsut had a pair of two almost 30-meter-high obelisks erected. Today, the tip of the southern one lies at the Holy Lake while the northern **Obelisk** ⓬ is still at its original position. The clear shading of color on the granite shows how high the stone covering of Tuthmosis III once was. Here too he also tried to extinguish at least the memory of the name of his hated predecessor, even though the golden tips of her obelisks continued to shine over Karnak.

Through the small, badly preserved **Sixth Pylon of Tuthmosis III** you reach the **Barque Sanctuary** ⓭. The two **Heraldic Pillars of Tuthmosis III** tower in front of it. The plants on the pillars are sculpted from the granite in the most classical severity of form: in the south (right) the lotus representing Upper Egypt, in the north (left) the papyrus representing Lower Egypt. To the left of the pillars two masterpieces from the time of Tutankhamen have been put on display again: (in part heavily restored) **Quartzite Statues** of Amen and Amaunet, Amen's consort in the myth of the creation of Hermopolis.

The **Granite Barque Shrine** was built in the name of Philip Arrhidaeus, the half brother of Alexander the Great on the site of an older chapel. It housed the sacred barque of Amen-Ra in which the image of the god was carried in only ceremonial barque processions.

On the other side of the **Court of the Middle Kingdom** ⓮, which today stands empty, is the **Festival Temple of Tuthmosis III**. One enters the shrine, laid out at right angles to the main axis, in the center of the hypostyle hall. Two statues mark the actual entrance ⓯ a little farther to the south. Immediately to the left of this is the chamber containing a copy of the famous **Karnak Tablet of the Kings** ⓰, which shows Tuthmosis III making an offering in front of 62 statues of his named ancestors (original in the Louvre). The unusual ground plan of this temple is dominated by a three-aisled hypostyle hall: 32 columns flank the slightly raised central aisle, which is supported by 20 columns resembling tent poles – a stone ceremonial tent unique to this temple. To the east of the hall of pillars is the **Botanical Garden** ⓱. Here you will see some fine high reliefs (only preserved in the lower section) in which Tuthmosis III had the flora and fauna he had seen during his military campaigns in the Middle East immortalized in an almost schoolbook-like fashion.

The **Holy Lake** ⓲ (200 x 117 meters) provided water for the priests' purification rites and served as the scene for ceremonial boat processions; or, unique to Karnak, as a pool for the sacred geese of Amen.

A passageway leads to the neighboring **Courtyard of the Seventh Pylon** ⓳. This is the beginning of the North-South Axis, a series of courtyards and gateways, reaching to the Tenth Pylon. Early in the

20th century a spectacular discovery was made in the court of the Seventh Pylon: more than 800 large stone figures and over 17,000 bronze statuettes were recovered from the *cachette*, an ancient store which had been set up in a "clearing up operation" in Ptolemaic times.

**THEBES WEST: The Realm of the Dead

Since the mid-1990s there has been a bridge over the Nile south of Luxor to **Thebes West**, but a river crossing by ferry is more elegant. From the landing stage the road leads through the fertile green fields and past idyllic hamlets. After a few kilometers you come to the edge of the desert and the heights of the western mountain range. Here is one of the largest necropolises in Egypt. It stretches for almost eight kilometers and its temples and tombs run on three levels, parallel to the edge of the fertile lands. The royal mortuary temples are on the plains, the private tombs on the mountain slopes, and finally, in the innermost and most secret zone, in the ravines and valleys of the rocky massif, are the burial grounds of the kings and queens, princes and princesses.

**Valley of the Kings

When Thebes became the capital of the newly united empire of the Pharaohs at the beginning of the Eighteenth Dynasty, the kings had their tombs also erected here; no longer in the form of pyramids, but as rock tombs in a hidden valley of the western mountains. But the pyramids, also the symbol of the immortal god-king, were not given up altogether: the almost 500-meter-high mountain summit of Al-Qurn dominates the **Valley of the Kings** ❺ like a natural pyramid. For almost 500 years, from the Eighteenth to the Twentieth Dynasty, the Pharaohs were buried here. Of more than

Right: Sunset over the Nile at Luxor.

60 tombs, 25 are royal burial places and the rest relatively simple shaft or chamber tombs of high officials. There was a commotion in the valley in 1922, when Howard Carter discovered the burial treasure of Tutankhamun, and again in 1995, when the American, Kent Weeks, found the entrance to the huge underground *gallery for the Princes of Ramses II*. Since then, it has not yet been possible to visit this tomb site, the largest hitherto known in Egypt, with its 108 tombs, but there is an excellent report about the site on the Internet (at the address www.kv5.com). Tombs which are open for viewing are:

★★Tomb of Tuthmosis' III.: The entrance to the tomb lies within a narrow rock crevice in the southernmost tip of the valley, and is easily accessible via steep iron steps. Steps and bridges lead through the roughly hewn, sloping portal to an entrance hall with a ceiling decoration depicting the star-studded night sky. On the walls you'll see lists of 741 deities and demons of the underworld. A stairway leads from here into an oval coffin

chamber, once again adorned with a ceiling of stars and also an outsized papyrus depiction. The twelve hours of the *Amduat* have been transferred onto the wall surface here, in the form of line drawings and hieroglyphics. To the right, behind the beautifully-reliefed quartzite sarcophagus of the Pharaoh, is the resurrection scene: The barque of the many-headed sun god is being pulled through the body of a snake, and the morning sun hovers just before the boundary of the underworld in the form of a scarab.

★ Tomb of Amenhotep II.: Like his father Tuthmosis III, Amenhotep II also had his burial chamber decorated with a ceiling of stars and the *Amduat*, a kind of "travel guide" for the world of the dead, intended to accompany the king, at the side of the sun god, to the resurrection. The ground plan, with exact right angles and straight lines, is different here, as is the decoration of the pillars. The king and the gods of the dead are portrayed here only in outline, yet with unbelievable perfection. In the lower part of the room is the quartzite sarcophagus in which the royal mummy was found, undamaged and decorated with flowers. In the side chambers, archeologists discovered 11 other royal mummies, brought here by the priest-kings of the Twenty-first Dynasty to protect them from grave robbers.

Tomb of Tutankhamen: If you have already seen the wealth of burial treasures of Tutankhamen in the Egyptian Museum in Cairo, you will be amazed at how small the most famous of all the tombs of the Valley of the Kings is. A corridor leads down into the antechamber, off which a small side chamber and burial chamber with a side room open. In the center of the burial chamber stands the open quartzite sarcophagus, with its three richly-ornamented coffins. In the largest of these the dead king rests. The pictures of the burial chamber show, on the east wall (right), the royal funeral procession. On the north wall (opposite) his successor Ay carries out the Mouth Opening Ceremony to bring his deceased predecessor back to life; in the middle, Tutankhamen is greeted by the sky goddess Nut, and beside this, Osiris is embraces the king.

Tomb of Horemheb: The tomb of the last king of the Eighteenth Dynasty is entered through a corridor running 105 meters deep into the mountain. The colored reliefs in two antechambers are among the finest in the whole valley. They show the king being accompanied by the gods into the interior of the tomb and bringing them offerings. The decoration of the burial chamber is incomplete, but it is for this very reason that it is so interesting: for the working methods of the artists can be clearly seen. They sketched texts and pictures in red color, and then made their corrections in black while others began to make the reliefs directly beside them.

Right: Bas-relief on one of the gilded shrines from the tomb of Tutankhamen (Egyptian Museum, Cairo).

Tomb of Seti I: The 100-meter-long tomb of the first important king of the Nineteenth Dynasty is famous for the unrivalled elegance of its fine reliefs. In the burial chamber, Giovanni Belzoni, who discovered the tomb, found the wonderful alabaster sarcophagus which today is to be seen in the Sir John Soane's Museum in London. The ceiling is decorated with astronomic motifs. Of the side rooms, the small chamber with the *Book of the Heavenly Cow* is especially interesting (to the right at the first pillar): Nut, the goddess of the sky, is portrayed here as a slender-limbed cow, with the barques of the sun god gliding along her body.

**Tomb of Ramses III.: With a length of 125 meters, this tomb is one of the largest in the Valley of the Kings. The reliefs have been well preserved in the upper chambers and the corridors, the first two of which are decorated with the *Litany of Ra* and with extracts from the *Amduat*. A total of 10 side chambers with rare and beautiful pictures lead from these corridors. The chambers on the right show mainly tomb offerings; on the left, scenes of offering and worship are portrayed. In the last chamber on the left is the famous (though damaged) picture of the two harp players, from which the tomb takes its epithet, the "Tomb of the Harpers." The neighboring hall bridges the deflection of the axis which was necessary when workers digging the corridors came across another tomb. On the walls are large paintings of gods and kings. The connecting series of rooms show mainly pictures of the nocturnal journey of the sun god through the underworld. The lower rooms have been badly damaged.

**Tomb of Ramses VI: The wonderful state of preservation of the colored reliefs and paintings make this tomb one of the climaxes of a visit to the Valley of the Kings. A flight of corridors and small rooms leads in a straight line into the interior of the mountain to the burial chamber. The side walls are decorated with

scenes from the *Amduat*, and the very similar *Book of Gates*; the ceiling paintings symbolize astronomical constellations. The most beautiful portrayals in this tomb are to be found in the decoration of the arched ceiling of the crypt: the long-limbed body of the goddess of the sky, Nut, can be seen twice – once in the form of the sky during the day, characterized by a single row of stars, and once as the night sky, through which the sun is traveling until it is reborn from the womb of the goddess in the morning.

**Valley of the Queens

In a picturesque neighboring valley in the extreme southernmost tip of the Theban western mountains is the *Place of Beauty*: the tombs of the queens, princes and princesses of the New Kingdom. Eighty tombs were found here in the **Valley of the Queens ❻** – more modest constructions than those of the kings, and sometimes even without wall decorations.

Tomb of Nefertari: The tomb of the wife of Ramses II is famous for the extraordinary beauty and artistic perfection of its colorful reliefs, which were restored in an exemplary project lasting six years. Since 1995 the tomb has been open for viewing.

A staircase leads down into the anteroom. As everywhere in the Valley of the Queens, the reliefs are cut into a layer of stucco which covers the somewhat crumbling limestone. On the left the wishes of the dead from the *Book of the Dead* are illustrated. Next to this you will see the mummy of the queen, with Isis and Nephthys as female falcons weeping over it. There is also the heavenly cow and six demons of the afterlife, who are armed with knives. Offerings were left on the ledge below. To the right in the neighboring chamber are wonderful representations of the queen and various gods. At the end of the corridor, under a picture of the winged goddess Maat, you will find the opening to the burial chamber with three side rooms.

**Tomb of Amen-her-khepeshef: This prince's tomb, with its beautifully-preserved stucco reliefs, is a main attraction in the Valley of the Queens. A staircase leads to a small anteroom, where the prince, always represented as a youth with a child's curls, is shown with his father Ramses III making offerings to the gods who accompany them further into the underworld. The individual portals are only opened to those who know the names of the terrible guards. Therefore, extracts from the 144th chapter of the Book of the Dead are painted on the walls as a magical aid to the little prince.

**Dair al-Madîna

In a valley basin, not far from the Valley of the Queens, lie the stone witnesses to a lucky archeological find: the village of artists and artisans who created the tombs of the Valley of the Kings and other important cemeteries in Thebes West. However, the French archeologists did not only stumble upon one of the few known settlements from Pharaonic times when they discovered ****Dair al-Madîna ❼**: by chance they also found a colorful chronicle of its inhabitants. In a "rubbish ditch" they unearthed around 5,000 *ostraka*, clay and limestone shards which had been used as sketch blocks, for notes, letter writing or report books. Approximately 40 to 60 artists and craftsmen lived in the village with their families. The slope in the west of the village became the artists' burial hill. Above the entrance to the rock chambers with their marvelous paintings, there were once places of worship which were crowned with small mud brick pyramids. As a rule, two of these tombs are open to the public:

**Tomb of Sennedjem: The tomb of the craftsman Sennedjem was found unplundered. Sennedjem belonged to the

Right: Relief featuring female musicians, from the Tomb of Rekhmire.

guild of the craftsmen of Dair al-Madîna as "a servant at the place of truth" in the Nineteenth Dynasty. The beautiful tomb furnishings are in the Egyptian Museum in Cairo (Upper Floor, Room 17). You descend a staircase into the vaulted burial chamber, which is painted all around with illustrations and texts from the *Book of the Dead*. The most famous row of scenes is that of the *Realms of the Blessed* on the narrow wall to the right, which shows the deceased and his wife in colorful pictures sowing and harvesting in the afterlife.

**Tomb of Inherkha: Almost directly opposite the tomb of Sennedjem is the Tomb of Inherkha, chief overseer of the craftsmen under the kings Ramses III and Ramses IV. The paintings of the lower of the two rock chambers are incredibly well preserved. The picture of the *Great Tomcat* – a symbol of the sun god Ra – shown destroying evil in the form of a serpent is particularly beautiful.

**Tombs of Sheikh 'Abd al-Qurna

Aristocrats, the kings' loyal advisors and high state officials, as well as lower-ranking Theban priests, artists and artisans – all could build their tombs with royal approval in the vicinity of their ruler. Together with countless undecorated shafts, some 450 private tombs have now been found in Thebes West which are decorated with paintings, and very occasionally with reliefs. Many of them are badly damaged, but the ****Tombs of Sheikh 'Abd al-Qurna ❽** are among the shining highlights of any visit to Egypt.

**Tomb of Rekhmire: The Tomb of Rekhmire, a vizier under Tuthmosis III, is an impressive complex high above the plain. The paintings in the transept illustrate his official duties as vizier. Of particular interest in the left wing are the portrayals of Asians, Nubians, inhabitants of the Land of Punt and Cretans. They are shown bringing their tributes, which include elephant tusks, ostrich eggs and feathers, beautiful vessels, incense trees

Luxor

and exotic animals, including giraffes, baboons, elephants, and even a brown bear. On the entrance wall of the right wing you will see a painting of a royal statue workshop, and opposite that a hunt in the desert. The long hall has an imposing sloped ceiling. The murals on the right show a banquet with many guests, beautiful servant girls and musicians. Opposite, various period workshops producing bricks, stone vessels, jewelry, statues and furniture have been depicted with careful attention to detail.

★★Tomb of Sennefer: A few steps above the tomb of Rekhmire is the tomb of Sennefer, who was mayor of Thebes during the time of Amenhotep II. The chambers of worship located above ground are not accessible, but Sennefer had his burial chamber designed in an unusually luxurious way. Visitors climb down 44 steps through a tunnel to the antechamber. Here, the unique creeping vine motifs which gave the tomb its nickname, the *Vine Arbor Tomb*, can be seen. On vines which seem to be rooted in the

floor of the chamber, splendid grapevines laden with fruit climb the walls and cover the ceiling, the uneven contours of which also represent the natural structure of a vine arbor.

★★Tomb of Nakht: The diminutive tomb of Nakht, temple astronomer and scribe during the reign of Tuthmosis IV, is perhaps one of the most beautiful rock tombs of the entire Land of the Nile. The paintings in the transept, on the left, show the entire agricultural cycle in great detail, from sowing to harvesting. The pink speckled effect of the false door was intended to magically transform it into a permanent place of worship made out of pink granite. But it is the scenes of the banquet next to it that bewitch the visitor, with its beautiful female musicians and graceful women, whose finely pleated dresses are colored gold by the melting cones of ointment they carry on their heads. In the right wing, Nakht and his wife can be seen sitting at an offering table, hunting in a papyrus thicket and on a bird hunt. The picture of the grape harvest

TEMPLES OF DAIR AL-BAHRÎ

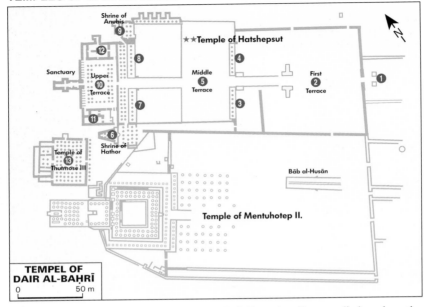

TEMPEL OF DAIR AL-BAḤRÎ

0   50 m

(on the narrow wall) is particularly attractive.

**Tomb of Menena: Menena was a contemporary of Nakht, which is immediately obvious from the similarity of the wall paintings. In the transept you can see the estate administrator and surveyor of the fields on the left, and at a banquet on the right. The first part of the long hall immortalizes the burial celebrations. Then, the judgement of the dead is shown (left), whereby the heart of the deceased is weighed against a statuette of Maat, the goddess of truth. Opposite this is a charming portrayal of a hunting scene in a papyrus thicket.

**Tomb of Ramose: The vizier of Amenhotep III and of his son Akhnaton had this true tomb palace built at the foot of the western mountains. It has a wide forecourt, a monumental hypostyle hall as a transept and a colonnade with its own chamber of worship in the form of a long

Right: Waiting for tourists at the entrance to the Temple of Hatshepsut.

hall. But when Ramose died work on the decoration of the walls of the anteroom had only just been begun. The reliefs show Ramose dressed in the apron of a vizier, which reached up to the armpits, in various scenes of sacrifice (right of the entrance) and in the circle of his loved ones at a festive banquet (left of the entrance). On the long wall the funeral procession moves towards the tomb, before which the mummy of the dead man has been placed for ritual acts. Directly below this the ramp leads to the underground burial chamber. The (partly incomplete) reliefs on the back wall are a unique example of Akhnaton's revolutionary rejection of the traditional conventions of style. The king appears on both sides of the (blocked) passageway to the long hall. On the left, portrayed in the traditional manner, he is shown sitting under a baldachin accepting Ramose's homage. But on the right the Amarna style has become dominant: under the rays of the sun god Aton, the king, accompanied by Nefertiti, is shown leaning out of the pal-

58

Inside the map:

Shrine of Anubis ⑨
★★Temple of Hatshepsut
⑫ ⑧
Sanctuary
Upper Terrace ⑩
⑤ Middle Terrace
④
First Terrace ② ①
③
⑦
⑪
⑥
Shrine of Hathor
Temple of Thutmose III ⑬
Bāb al-Husān
Temple of Mentuhotep II.

ace window down to Ramose. The vizier, richly bedecked in necklaces of the gold of honor, is being enthusiastically fêted by the courtiers.

★★Temples of Dair al-Bahrî

A 300-meter-high, semicircular rock basin surrounds the **★★Temples of Dair al-Bahrî 9**: the oldest structure, the **Mortuary Temple of Mentuhotep II**, is badly damaged and closed to visitors.

North of it you can visit the **★★Terrace Temple of Hatshepsut**, an architectural masterpiece. The road which leads from the fertile lands to the temple follows the course of the ancient processional path, once an avenue of more than 100 sandstone sphinxes. The gate, now completely in ruins, was flanked by two persea trees in Hatsheput's time. The stumps of the 3,500 year old trees can still be seen in the **tree hollow 1** where they are (rather poorly) protected by fences.

The **Lower Terrace 2** is, strictly speaking, the forecourt of the temple, but there is little there to remind you of the once blooming garden and papyrus plants. On both sides of the ramp the façade of the Central Terrace is formed by a colonnade. The (badly preserved) reliefs **3 / 4** show on the left the transportation of a pair of obelisks from Aswân to Thebes, and on the right the queen hunting in a papyrus thicket.

Two chapels flank the pillared aisles on the **Central Terrace 5**: on the right stands the Chapel of Anubis; on the left stands the small **Sanctuary of Hathor 6**, a rock grotto with a hall of pillars. The Hathoric capitals of the pillars are gracefully carved. They show the goddess' countenance (from the front!) depicting her with the ears of a cow. The delicate wall reliefs, by comparison, show Hathor in the form of a cow.

The most famous scenes in the temple show an expedition to the "frankincense country" of Punt, and which today is be-

Luxor

lieved to have been in eastern Sudan and northern Eritrea. The narrow wall of the **Punt Hall 7** shows the Egyptian delegation being greeted by the inhabitants of Punt and their princess (whose voluptuous figure seems to be less a picture of illness and more an ideal of fertility). They are also shown exchanging Egyptian daggers, chains and gold for frankincense trees and elephant tusks.

The relief cycle in the **Birth Hall 8** shows Hatshepsut's divine origins (this can only be clearly made out in the morning light). From left to right the scenes show: Amen with the queen mother Ahmose holding hands on a bed; Amen in front of the ram-headed Khnum, who is making the queen and her Ka (portrayed as a young boy!) on the potter's wheel; Thot making the announcement to Ahmose of the birth of her divine child; and finally the pregnant Ahmose on her way to the Birth Hall.

The colorful reliefs of the **Anubis Chapel 9** have been extremely well preserved. The richly-set banquet tables for

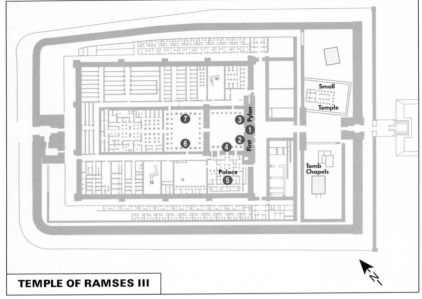

TEMPLE OF RAMSES III

the gods on the rear wall of the columned anteroom are particularly beautiful.

The **Upper Terrace** ❿ (not accessible) consists of an open columned court in front of the central sanctuary of Amen, **side rooms** ⓫ for the worship of the dead queen and her father, and a **sacrificial courtyard** ⓬ for the worship of the sun.

The remains of a third sanctuary in Dair al-Bahrî were discovered only in the 1960's, namely the **Temple of Tuthmosis III** ⓭, from which wonderful reliefs could be saved (Luxor Museum) despite it having been destroyed by a landslide in ancient times and later used as a quarry.

The **Ramesseum

The "Tomb of Ozymandias," as the Roman author Diodorus called the **Ramesseum** ❿ – the mortuary temple of Ramses II, is surely one of the most fascinating temple ruins in Thebes West.

Right: The broken granite colossus in the Ramesseum.

Huge blocks and fragments of statues lie spread around the grounds, as if scattered there by the hand of a titan; a row of enormous Osirian pillars tower like a mysterious memorial above the whole area. And all this is set against the imposing backdrop of the tomb mountain of Sheikh 'Abd al-Qurna.

On the other hand, the temple architecture – even including some of the relief decoration – is in such fine condition that you can easily get a good impression of their original splendor.

Scenes on the great **Entrance Pylon** once again celebrate the Syrian wars of the great Ramses (on the north tower, left), in particular the Battle of Kadesh (on the south tower, right). The steps to the Second Pylon, of which today only the north tower still stands, were once flanked by two 17.5-meter-high **granite colossi**. One of these gigantic seated figures is still there, though broken into huge pieces of gargantuan proportions. One index finger alone is a full meter long, and the chest measures seven meters!

Luxor

The **Second Pylon**, too, shows Ramses on a chariot as the hero of Kadesh, storming the ill-fated fortress surrounded by the river Orontes. In the west of the Second Courtyard is a **colonnade** made of two rows of Osirian pillars and papyrus-shaped columns. This forms the façade of the once covered temple building, which begins at the hypostyle hall.

Beautiful reliefs can be seen on the walls of the small neighboring **Eight-pillared Hall**, especially those on the back wall to the right are of interest. Ramses is sitting in front of the *ished* tree of the god Atum of Heliopolis who, with the scribe goddess Seshat and Thot, is writing the name of the king on the leaves of the sacred tree, thereby ensuring the ruler a long and happy reign – even in the afterlife. The further temple rooms have been destroyed.

****Madînat Hâbû**

The southernmost of the "Houses of Millions of Years," as the ancient Egyp-

tians optimistically called the temples of their dead kings, is the ****Mortuary Temple of Ramses III in Madînat Hâbû** ⓫. A double ring wall surrounds the huge temple area, the center of which is the mortuary temple of the last great king (1189–1158 BC) of the new Kingdom. Even though the temple in some respects could be considered almost a copy of the Ramesseum, the fortress-like entrance is unique in Egyptian architecture.

On both towers of the **First Pylon** ❶ the king is portrayed in a traditional pose of triumph, slaying his enemies. The great opponents of Ramses III were the Libyans and the sea peoples, an alliance of various tribes of Asia Minor. The victories of the Egyptians in these battles are the subjects of the first courtyard, whose **pictures** and **inscriptions** ❷ / ❸ celebrate Ramses as a war hero. On the back of the pylon he is shown in a chariot or consulting with his generals, who verify the numbers of the enemies they have killed by means of their amputated hands and penises.

Behind the **balcony** ❹ in the south wall of the courtyard are the remains of a small **palace** ❺ where the king and his court lived during festivals – in this life and the next. The **reliefs** ❻ / ❼ of the Second Courtyard are dedicated to such temple festivals: in the south a feast in honor of Sokar, god of the dead in Memphis, and in the north the feast of the fertility god Min, a harvest festival at whose center is a procession of the idol led by a white bull, Min's sacred animal. Of the connecting rooms, the hypostyle hall and a succession of chambers of worship, only portions of the lower walls and the stumps of columns remain. Around the temple one can see the mud brick ruins of household buildings, stores and living quarters of this place of worship, which was also later settled by Christians and Copts and was not abandonded until the the ninth century AD.

★★Colossi of Memnon

In the middle of the fertile lands are two gigantic seated figures of quartzite: the **★★Colossi of Memnon** ⓬, the legendary king who killed Achilles before Troy – at least that is who the Greeks thought these almost 18-meter-high statues of Amenhotep III were. At one point in time these monoliths used to guard the gate to his mortuary temple, of which, unfortunately, little otherwise remains. The legend of the song of Memnon, with which he greeted his mother Eos – the goddess of the dawn – every morning, made the colossi a much-visited wonder of the world, even back in ancient times. The mysterious singing, which could be heard here at sunrise, was more than likely due to the warming effect of the sun's rays on the rock and the resulting tension produced therein. It was only silenced when the northern statue, the torso of which was split apart by the earthquake of 27 BC, was restored some 200 years later.

LUXOR (☎ 095)

🛈 **Tourist Bazaar**, beside the New Winter Palace Hotel, tel. 372215; and at the airport, tel. 383294.

🖼 *GETTING THERE:* Numerous international **Schedule and Charter Airlines** fly directly to Luxor, *Egypt Air* flies to Luxor from Cairo several times daily. Luxor is accessible from all of the larger towns in the Nile valley, via **railway**. There are trains commuting several times a day along the Cairo – Luxor – Aswân route.

Buses operated by the *Upper Egypt Bus Company* have four daily runs from Cairo bus station to Luxor, and they stop en route in all of the larger Nile valley towns. If you wish to travel by means of a luxury bus, make sure to buy your ticket at least one day in advance at the bus station. For the Red Sea coast, buses operate between Hurghada and Luxor several times daily. Out of security reasons, however, these trips are currently only being undertaken with military escorts.

🛏 ⊛⊛⊛ *City center:* **Mercure Etap Luxor**, Corniche an-Nîl, tel. 380944, fax 374912. **Mercure Inn Egotel**, 10 Sh. Ma'bad Luxor, tel. 373521, fax 370051. **Novotel Luxor**, Sh. Khâlid Ibn al-Walîd, tel. 580923, fax 380972. **Sofitel Winter Palace** and **New Winter Palace**, Corniche an-Nîl, tel. 380422/23, fax 374087. *Stadtrand:* **Luxor Hilton**, New Karnak, tel. 374933, fax 376571. **Belladona Resort Club Mediterranée**, Sh. Khâlid Ibn al-Walîd, tel. 380850, fax 380879. **Isis**, Sh. Khâlid Ibn al-Walîd, tel. 372750, fax 372923. **Luxor Sheraton**, Sh. Khâlid Ibn al-Walîd, tel. 374544, fax 374941. **Jolie Ville Moevenpick**, Crocodile Island, tel. 374855, fax 374936. ⊛⊛ *City center:* **Luxor Hotel**, at the Temple of Luxor, tel. 380018, fax 380017. **Mina Palace**, Corniche an-Nîl, tel. 372074. **New Emilio**, Sh. Yûsuf Hasan, tel. 371601, fax 374884. **Philippe**, Sh. Dr. Labîb Habashî, tel. 372284, fax 380060. ⊛ *City center:* **New Windsor**, Sh. Nefertiti, tel. 374306, fax 373447. **Pyramids**, Sh. Yûsuf Hasan, tel. 373243. **Beau Soleil**, Sh. Salâh ad-Dîn, 372671. **Sphinx**, Sh. Yûsuf Hasan, tel. 372830. **Venus**, Sh. Yûsuf Hasan, tel. 372625.

🍴 Excellent restaurants, serving both oriental and international cuisine, can be found in the following hotels: **Mercure Etap, Luxor Hilton, Luxor Sheraton** and **Jolie Ville Moevenpick**. More simple restaurants serving oriental dishes are situated behind the Temple of Luxor and around the station. Also recommended are: the **restaurant in the Mina Palace Hotel**, Corniche an-Nîl; the **Marhaba restaurant** with its beautiful terrace offering views of the Nile valley, Luxor Tourist Bazaar; for small snacks try the **Terrace**

Café of the **Mercure Etap Luxor Hotel**, Corniche an-Nîl.

Discotheques (in the western sense) are in the following hotels: Luxor Hilton and Mercure Etap Luxor. The **nightclubs** of the Old Winter Palace and Isis hotels feature live music and belly-dancing (international folklore is also available in the Isis Hotel). The **Jolie Ville Moevenpick** organizes *Oriental Dinners* with belly-dancing and folklore.

Museum of Luxor, Corniche an-Nîl. daily 9 am-12 pm and 4-9 pm, in summertime from 10 am-1 pm and 5-10 pm; an extra fee is charged for the room featuring the statue store found in the Temple of Luxor.

Museum of Mummification Techniques, Corniche an-Nîl, the opening hours are the same as for the Museum of Luxor.

CITY TRANSPORTATION: The main means of inner-city transportation are **taxis** and **carriages**. So that you can make better deals with the drivers, make sure you find out the official tariffs in your hotel, which should be able to provide you with this information. The coach drivers of Luxor still retain their ancient reputation as a bunch of swindlers!

Since there is no longer a bridge in the south of Luxor, tourist ferries no longer operate. But travelers can take the **local ferry**. It's located opposite the Mina Palace Hotel. There is a taxi and group taxi stand at the landing quay on the western shore. Make sure you arrange the price for a day trip or half-day trip *before* departure!

Bicycles can be hired at the following hotels: *Mercure Etap Luxor* and *Jolie Ville Moevenpick*. Those cycling to Thebes West should take the temperature into account. Toward the Valley of the Kings, be aware that several kilometers of the journey traverse a very hot valley basin which is gently sloped, uphill.

SIGHTS: **Luxor by night** – the Temple of Luxor is atmospherically floodlit and open to visitors every evening from 6:30 pm until 9 pm.

ACTIVITIES: **Horseback riding** on beautiful Arab horses in the western desert – information is available at the „Discovery Desks" in all the larger hotels. **Sailing** on the Nile and to Banana Island – a peninsula with lush banana plantations; **Hot-air balloon rides** over the Nile valley; **swimming** is always an option – even if you're not a hotel guest – entrance fees charged for this in the Mercure Etap Luxor, Winter Palace and Isis hotels.

DAY TRIPS: You can book a bus trip to the **Temple of Dandara** at most travel agents. The buses depart at set times – in convoys protected by military escorts. At the present time, tours to the **Temple of Abydos** are available again. This is located about 180 km to the north and these trips can be combined with sightseeing at Dandara. There are also convoys which head farther

south to the **Temples of Edfu** and **Kôm Ombo**, and they depart twice daily.

KARNAK (☎ 095)

Horus, Sh. Ma'bad Karnak, tel. 372165. **Nefertiti**, Sh. Ma'bad Karnak, tel. 372386. **Youth Hostel**, 16 Sh. Ma'bad Karnak, tel. 372139.

Open-air Museum, Temple of Karnak, 8 am-5 pm.

SIGHTS: **Karnak by night** – a light and sound show takes places in the temple daily, at 6 pm (in the summer at 6:30 pm) and 7:30 pm (summer 8 pm), in different languages. Half of the time is spent walking through the temple to the large columned hall, the rest of the time is spent in the stands at the holy lake. Make sure to bring a jacket and a pocket torch.

THEBES WEST (☎ 095)

Abdul Kassem, beside the Temple of Seti I., tel. 310319. **Dream Valley**, off Madînat Hâbû, tel. 310581. **El-Geziza**, near the ferry dock, tel. 310034. **Pharao Hotel**, behind the antiquities inspectorate near Madînat Hâbû, tel. 374924. **Hotel Marsam**, behind the Kolossi of Memnon, tel. 372403.

Opening hours: As a rule, all sights are open from 6:30 am to 6 pm, and in winter until 5 pm. One exception is the Tomb of Nefertari in the **Valley of the Queens**, which is open in winter from 8:30 am-4 pm, summer from 7:30 am-2 pm (closed from 12-1 pm).

Tips: Any entrance tickets for Thebes West can **only** be purchased at the ticket desk by the *Inspectorate for Antiquities* (at the intersection behind the Colossi of Memnon). In the Valley of the Kings, at the present time, only three tombs may be visited per day. Despite the high entrance fee of 100 LE per ticket, the Tomb of Nefertari may only be viewed for a period of 10 minutes. Furthermore, only 150 tickets are sold per day. Therefore it is advisable to start queueing at the ticket desk quite early in the morning to avoid disappointment (it is open from 6 am).

At the ticket desk you can also obtain a photography permit or permit for video/film recordings in the tombs (without a flash!). Those without a permit will be required to leave their equipment at the entrance. Make sure you take a pocket flashlight for the tombs.

DAY TRIPS: The one-hour **mountain hike** from the Valley of the Kings to the Temple of Dair al-Bahrî will surely turn out to be a memorable experience. The hiking path is easy to find and is popular with pedlars, who like to help travelers with directions. For day trips to Thebes West or an easy **ride** through the sugar cane fields, donkeys can be hired, escorted by a local guide.

FROM LUXOR
TO THE
NUBIAN TEMPLES

UPPER NILE VALLEY

EDFU

KÔM OMBO

ASWÂN

THE NUBIAN TEMPLES

UPPER NILE VALLEY

The most romantic, though somewhat uncomfortable, way to cover the 220 kilometers between Luxor and Aswân is without doubt in a *feluka*. These large sailing boats are today, as they have been for thousands of years, the main method of transport on the Nile – at least south of Cairo. A luxurious alternative is a cruise on one of the elegant floating hotels which anchor at the temples of Edfu and Kôm Ombo.

EDFU

Edfu ❶ (Arabic: *Idfû*) is a small district town in Egypt's southernmost province, Aswân. From a distance you can already see the huge pylons of the **★★Temple of Horus** towering above the houses on the west bank, to which a wide bridge leads across the river.

The history of Edfu dates back to the Old Kingdom, and perhaps even further back than that. Today the ancient town is in ruins – it is buried under the houses of the modern town and in the piles of rubble to the west of the temple. But the temple itself, which was dedicated to the falcon god Horus, is one of the best preserved

Left: Making sail on a Nile feluka.

temples of Pharaonic Egypt. Work on this structure began in August 237 BC, under the rule of Ptolemy III, and was finished 180 years later under Ptolemy XII, Cleopatra's father. Older buildings had previously been torn down; only to the east of the First Pylon you can still see the foundations of a temple gate from the time of Ramses II.

The façade of the immense **First Pylon ❶** (79 meters high, 36 meters wide) shows Ptolemy XII in the traditional pose, *Slaying the Enemies*, in front of the main temple gods, Horus and Hathor, who was worshiped in Edfu as the consort of the falcon god. Four deep longitudinal niches in the wall, with two square openings above each one, served as anchors for huge flag poles which protruded from the gate towers. A splendid winged sun, one of the many forms of Horus of Edfu, decorates the groove above the portal; two granite falcons stand on guard in front of it.

The **Great Court ❷** is surrounded on three sides by a colonnade with 32 columns, which are formed in a wide variety of stylized plant capitals. The **paintings on the walls ❸** / **❹** illustrate scenes of sacrificial offerings and rituals, and also the coronation of the king: to the left you can see the Pharaoh wearing the crown of Lower Egypt, on the right, with the tiara

Southern Egypt

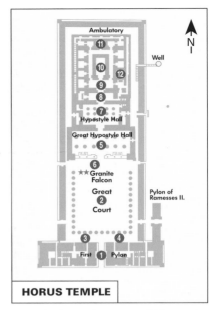

HORUS TEMPLE

of Upper Egypt. At the bottom of each one a boat procession is shown which alludes to the *Holy Wedding* of the pair of gods. Every year the statue of Hathor set off in a splendid convoy to travel the 160 kilometers from Dandara to Edfu to visit her divine husband.

You enter the temple through the **Great Hypostyle Hall** ❺ which lies in semi-darkness behind stone gates decorated with reliefs. In front of them is the symbol of Edfu: the famous ****granite falcon** ❻ with the double crown.

Through a second **Hypostyle Hall** ❼ and two anterooms, in which the **offering tables** ❽ and the **shrines of visiting deities** ❾ once stood, you come to the center of the house of the gods. The **Holy of Holies** ❿, a shrine with a shimmering cultic image located at the mythical border between heaven and earth, is surrounded by a circle of chapels. A granite pedestal for the wooden barque of the god

Above: The symbol of Edfu – the famous granite falcon.

stands in front of the monolithic granite shrine. On the walls you can see the king, here Ptolemy IV, offering incense in front of the barques of Horus (left) and Hathor (right). A **copy of a barque** ⓫ has been placed in the chamber behind the Holy of Holies.

The ceiling of the **New Year's Chapel** ⓬ is particularly beautiful. It depicts the goddess of the sky, Nut, and the 12 phases of the course of the sun in the form of a barque journey. After the first rites of the New Year's Festival the priests went in procession from here to the temple roof.

KÔM OMBO

At the southern edge of the small towm Kôm Ombo ❷ the road forks right to the ****Temple of Kôm Ombo**, which has a marvelous location, situated on a hill directly beside the Nile. Because the temple, begun in the second century BC, is dedicated to two major deities, the ancient architects simply built two parallel processional paths (instead of the usual

one) through the temple halls to two
sanctuaries standing side by side: the left
side dedicated to the falcon-headed
Harwer (Horus the Elder), and the right
side to the crocodile god Sobek. Access
to the **Great Court** is through the **First
Pylon**, of which only the foundation
walls are still standing. A colonnade of
16 columns with colorful reliefs from the
time of Tiberius joins the splendid pillar
walls in front of the covered temple building. In the **Great Hypostyle Hall**, in addition to the wonderful plant capitals, the
reliefs on the left are well worth looking
at. They show the king in the company of
various gods. Through three small anterooms you come to the Holy of Holies,
which is divided into two parts and with
the exception of the foundation walls has
been completely destroyed. The most famous picture in the temple, the *Medical
Relief*, is on the back wall of the outer am-
bulatory: Trajan (only the lower body still
exists) kneels before the gods, offering
them medical instruments, including for-
ceps, scalpels and suckers and healing
amulets.

After a few kilometers the road to
Aswân, 40 kilometers away, passes close
to *Darâw ❸, where every Tuesday a
camel market takes place, to which large
caravans travel up from the Sudan. The
closer you get to Aswân, the more African the landscape appears to become.

**ASWÂN

For many travelers **Aswân ❹ is the
most beautiful town in the entire Nile Valley. On the west bank its fairy-tale scenery of yellow sand dunes sweeping down
to the deep blue waters of the Nile, out of
which rise the dark scattered shapes of
granite crags, is unforgettable. These
massive shapes of worn rock almost look
like elephants.

The southernmost town in Egypt is the
administrative center of the Province of
Aswân, which stretches from Edfu to the

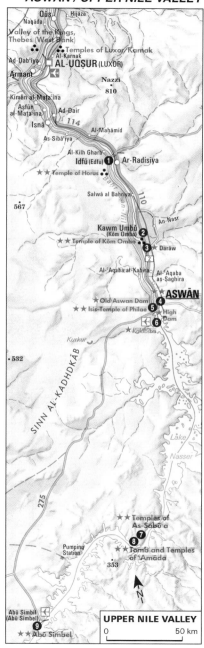

Sudanese border. Ethnically speaking, Aswân belongs to Nubia, a cultural area which reaches to the sixth cataract at Khartûm in the Sudan.

Despite the fact that the dark skinned Nubians have long been "Arabized," whole villages still maintain the Nubian culture and traditions, including the languages, Kenuzi and Mahasi.

Today, around 500,000 people live in Aswân. The economic upswing, brought by the new dam, can be felt everywhere, but this has by no means reached the planned dimensions. The real "city" consists of only two streets: the well-kept **Corniche** ❶ along the Nile, approximately two kilometers in length, with its string of shops and several coffee houses, and the parallel *bazaar street ❷ (Shâri 'Abbâs Farîd/Shâri as-Sûq). In addition, Aswân has more than its share of sights, the first which should be mentioned being the **Nubian Museum** ❸ which, in a

generously planned exhibition area at the southern edge of the town, offers a unique survey of the history and culture of Nubia from prehistoric times to the Islamic era.

*Elephantine Island

Abu, the southernmost border town of ancient Egypt, developed in Pharaonic times at the southern tip of * **Elephantine** ❹, a 1.5-kilometer-long island. One of the most impressive relics of Elephantine is the ancient *Nilometer not far from the museum. It consists of a sloping stair shaft which leads down to the Nile. The water level of the river was measured on the scale chiseled into the sides. The white marble tablets show that the Nilometer, which dates from Roman times, was restored in the last century. The consistently low water level of the Nile since the construction of the High Dam, however, have rendered this old instrument obsolete.

The monumental terrace-like arrangement of the **wharf**, which was restored in

Above: A sailing party to the Mausoleum of the Aga Khân.

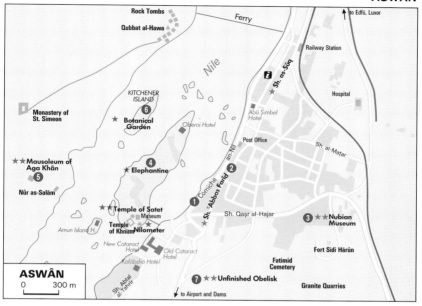

Southern Egypt

Roman times, can be seen in front of the **Temple of Khnum**, the ram-headed god. The temple forms the uppermost plateau of a mound of ruins in the middle of decayed mud brick buildings. Only a **granite gate** decorated with reliefs and a huge fallen **granite shrine** farther to the west suggest just how imposing the Thirtieth Dynasty temple must once have been. To the north and a little farther down stands – once again – the **★★Temple of Satet**, Khnum's divine consort. The small peripteros from the time of Hatshepsut has been reconstructed in its original size on a huge reinforced concrete slab; under it is an archaic sacrificial altar which stands in front of two gigantic, polished granite rocks.

Opposite Elephantine Island the **★★Mausoleum of the Aga Khân ❺** towers high above the Nile, and above the white villa of the Begûm, which has the rather poetic name of *Nûr as-Salâm* ("Light of Peace"). A wide path leads up to the tomb of the one-time leader of the Ismailite Hodshas, who was revered as a

divinely-inspired Imâm by the four million believers of his sect.

From up here there is a fine panoramic view of the whole area of the First Cataract, right up to the High Dam eight kilometers farther to the south. To the north, the red iron mountains of Aswân glow in the distance, and there, where white sails conglomerate, the harbor of **Kitchener Island ❻** can be made out. In the days of the British protectorate the little island belonged to the British Consul General, Lord Kitchener whose palm garden formed the basis for the wonderful **★Botanical Gardens** later established here by the Egyptian government.

Granite Quarries

The **granite quarries** which, throughout Egyptian history, supplied the Pharaohs with valuable materials for their vessels, statues, sarcophagi, obelisks, religious shrines and special features for their temples and tomb complexes, are situated southeast of Aswân.

The main attraction of the pink granite quarries is the **★★Unfinished Obelisk ❼**, dating back to the 15th century BC, to the time of Queen Hatshepsut. This gigantic monolith, thought to weigh some 1,168 tons, would have become the largest obelisk in Egypt with its height of 42 meters and base area of 4.2 x 4.2 meters, but the ambitious plan was thwarted when the stone developed cracks. Another attempt to carve a smaller obelisk out of the same block also failed for the same reason.

The Dams

To the south of Aswân are the two great dams of Lake Nasser at the first cataract. The **★Old Aswân Dam** was built between 1898 and 1902 by English engineers. The two-kilometer-long granite dam wall was enlarged twice and is now 51 meters high, 35 meters along its base, and 12 meters wide at the top and has 180 sluice gates.

Above: A Nubian girl. Right: The Temple of Isis at Philae.

As the rapid population growth made the establishment of new agricultural areas, in order to meet food requirements, increasingly urgent, the **★★Sadd al-'âlî High Dam** was built eight kilometers south of the old dam, with the aid of Soviet credit and engineers. For 11 years (1960–1971) 33,000 Egyptians and 1,900 Russians worked on this mammoth project which cost approximately US$2.5-million.

The earthquake-proof concrete dam is formed by a 111-meter-high curved structure. It is 3.6 kilometers long, 980 meters wide at the bottom and 40 meters wide at the top. The interior of this giant is made up of 35 percent sand, 55 percent rough rock and 10 percent clay. The center of the dam over the 520-meter-wide river bed is formed by a huge clay core. This spreads farther into an injected insulating apron of clay, cement, silicate and aluminate, which reaches 44 meters below the bottom of the dam.

The reservoir in which the Nile floodwaters are stored throughout the year is 500 kilometers long and 200 kilometers wide, and has a surface area of 5000 square kilometers. If the water ever reaches the maximum planned level of 182 meters above sea level (14 meters below the top of the reservoir), it will have reached its maximum water capacity of 164 billion cubic meters. Of these, 30 billion cubic meters would be made up of silt deposits, 90 billion cubic meters would be the normal water storage capacity, and 44 billion cubic meters constitute the flood safety margin.

THE NUBIAN TEMPLES

The enormous reservoir threatened not only the homes of 100,000 Nubians who had to be resettled, but also their cultural heritage of several millenia. With the help of UNESCO a unique international project began in 1960 in which countless scientists and specialists from all over the

Southern Egypt

world participated in the relocation of 22 monuments to a safer place, rebuilding them exactly in their original state.

The northernmost of these is the Ptolomaic ★★**Temple of Isis**, on the Island of **Philae ❺** (actually *Agílkia*, but the name of the original island is more common). Below the old dam is the landing stage for the boat which chugs past the bizarre granite formations to the entrance at the south of the island.

The **First Pylon of the Temple of Isis** shows Ptolemy XII *Slaying the Enemies* and making sacrifices to the gods. As the last Ptolemaic builder, the father of the renowned Cleopatra finished the work which had been begun under Ptolemy II a good 200 years before (third century BC). The **Great Court** is bordered to the east by a colonnade and by chambers for the priests, and in the west by the **Birth House** with its beautiful colonnade. The theme of the murals inside the chapel is the birth of Horus, who was hidden from Seth by his mother Isis in the swamps of the Delta where he was brought up. The

back wall of the innermost chamber illustrates this with a picture of the Horus falcon in the center of a graphically fanned-out sheaf of papyrus.

The **Second Pylon**, with scenes of Ptolemy XII making offerings, leads, with a change in the direction of the axis, to the Hypostyle Hall which served as a church in Christian times. Passing through several small halls you come to the **Holy of Holies** which has some wonderful large reliefs of the king before the gods and the stand for the cultic barque of Isis.

Of the buildings in the north of the island, only the Roman city gate was moved. There are charming reliefs on the columns in the forecourt of the **Temple of Hathor** (second century BC) on the east bank: monkeys playing instruments and the god Bes playing the tambourine. Beside it is the **Kiosk of Trajan**, a stone baldachin with wonderful plant pillars; it may have been a shrine for the divine barque in the period of the Roman emperors.

Beyond Sadd al-'âlî the granite plateau of *New Kalâbsha ❻ lies like a museum island in a reservoir which can only be reached by boat (the landing stage is below the dam monument). The center of the complex is the *Temple of the God Mandulis which, in 1962/63, thanks to financial assistance from Germany, became the first Nubian temple to be moved here from its original position in Kalâbsha, ancient *Talmis*, almost 40 kilometers further south. It had been built there by Caesar Augustus to commemorate his victory on the southern border of the newly won province of Egypt.

From the roof of the temple you will find a wonderful view of the bizarre "moonscape" of the lake shore and the *Kiosk of Qertassi, a small columned chapel built in Greco-Roman times next to the sandstone quarries of Qertassi near Kalâbsha and which was brought here

Above: Power and might of a Pharaoh – the colossus of Ramses II in front of the Great Temple of Abû Simbel.

even before the Temple of Mandulis. On the "outskirts" of Old Kalâbsha there was also the small **Rock Temple of Bait al-Wâlî, which has been rebuilt only 100 meters from the Temple of Mandulis. The beautiful reliefs of this temple – the most northern of the seven Nubian temples of Ramses II which still retain some of their original coloring – celebrate the Pharaoh as a victorious military leader.

Even though approach roads to the temples of New Sabû'a and New Amâda have long been planned, at present the only way, albeit a very pleasant one, to visit them is by taking a cruise of several days length on Lake Nasser, from Aswân to Abû Simbel. The ship docks on the west bank of the reservoir in **New Sabû'a ❼, about 160 kilometers south of Sadd al-'âlî. In New Sabû'a there are three impressive structures which you can visit: a *Temple of Ramses II, which was transported from the flooded Wâdî as-Sabû'a, four kilometers away; the *Temple of Ad-Dakka, a Ptolemaic-Roman construction which was begun by

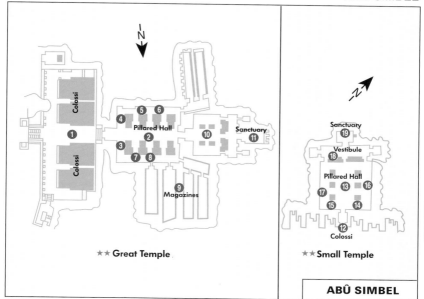

★★ Great Temple

★★ Small Temple

Southern Egypt

the Nubian King Ergamenes in the third century BC; and the **★Temple of Serapis** dating from the late Roman period which was originally situated 35 kilometers to the south at Al-Maharraqa, on the border between the Roman territory and the Nubian kingdom of Meroe.

Forty kilometers south of New-Sebû'a, in **★★New 'Amâda ❽**, three further monuments were re-erected in extensive salvage projects: the **Rock Temple of Ramses II** from Ad-Derr; the **★Rock Tomb of Pennut** from Aniba, where the administrators of Lower Nubia served during the Twentieth Dynasty; and the **★★Temple of Tuthmosis III** from 'Amâda, which in a unique project, was drawn, without being dismantled, along 2.6 kilometers of track to a new site, 65 meters higher than its first location. The reliefs in the Shrine of Amen-Re from the 15th century BC are well-preserved, thanks to the shrine having been converted into a church. To deprive the heathen pictures of their power the Christians covered them with a layer of mortar.

The Miracle of ★★Abû Simbel

Those who do not come to the **★★Temples of Abû Simbel ❾** by cruise ship or plane can take the asphalt highway leading south to the Sudan. Straight as a die it cuts its way through the desert, parallel to the caravan route along which Sudanese camels are driven to the market held every weekend in Darâw.

The salvaging of the two rock temples of Abû Simbel was truly a project of superlatives. The sacred mountains were moved 180 meters farther away from the lake and to an elevation 64 meters higher. They were sawn into more than one thousand blocks, weighing up to 30 tons each, and were rebuilt on their original east-west axis, exactly as before. Today, a gigantic concrete dome arches over both of the "inner" rock chambers and supports the artificial mountain built over the top. (This can be seen at the Great Temple.) The work took three years to complete (1965–68) and the total cost amounted to US \$42 million.

Like a petrified demonstration of power, the four 20-meter-high **seated statues of Ramses II** ❶ tower majestically in front of the rock pylons of the ****Great Temple**. The standing figures of the royal women and children are also larger than life. High above you will see a frieze with 22 baboons praying with arms raised to the sun. Twice a year – around February 20 and October 20 – the rays of the sun reach right into the sanctuary 64 meters down into the rock, in order to "unite with the holy statues of the great gods": Amen, Ra and Ptah, and in their midst apears the king himself!

Here in Nubia, Ramses appears as the god of all gods – a form of existence otherwise only attributed to the dead Pharaoh. And so Ramses is shown worshiping himself in the niche above the portal, where he brings the falcon-headed sun god Ra-Harakhti an offering. The huge sculpture is part of a "pictorial puzzle"

Above: The Lesser Temple of Abû Simbel.

symbolizing the throne name of the king.

The interior rooms of the temple begin with the **Pillared Hall** ❷. Its central aisle is flanked by eight 10-meter-high statues of the king. The colorful wall reliefs once again celebrate the courage of the great Ramses. Beside the traditional reliefs depicting the **Slaying of the Enemies**, portrayed as **Asians** ❸ on the right and **Nubians** ❹ on the left (also symbolizing the geographical location of these two peoples), the king is shown storming a Syrian fortress, lancing a Libyan, in a triumphal procession with **Nubian prisoners** ❺ / ❻ and in the various phases of the famous **Battle of Kadesh** against the Hittites ❼ / ❽.

The side chambers were **storerooms** ❾ for the instruments of worship and the temple treasures. Through the small **Four-Pillared Hall** ❿, showing scenes of sacrifice in front of the divine barques, you enter the transept and the **Holy of Holies** ⓫. Here, there are large sculptures of Ptah (left), of Amen wearing the high feathered crown, of the king, and of the sun falcon Ra-Harakhti.

The ****Lesser Temple** was dedicated by Ramses II to his favorite wife, Nefertari, and the goddess Hathor, with whom the queen is always identified: for example in the **Colossi** ⓬ on the façade where she is surrounded by statues of her husband, the beautiful Nefertari is shown with the horned crown of the goddess.

The **interior** ⓭ is divided up by six pillars decorated with Hathoric heads. In the center of the fine, well-preserved reliefs are the triumphs over his enemies ⓮ / ⓯, scenes of sacrifice ⓰ and the coronation of the king ⓱. The coronation of Nefertari by the goddesses Isis and Hathor is particularly gracefully portrayed (diagonal hall at ⓲). Although somewhat weathered, the cult statue in the **Holy of Holies** ⓳ can be made out well: it is a raised relief of the cow goddess Hathor-Nefertari, protecting a statuette of Ramses II.

BETWEEN LUXOR AND ASWÂN

Edfu and **Kôm Ombo** are usually conveniently visited during a trip from Luxor to Aswân. Organized day trips by bus or taxi to the temples can be booked in Luxor as well as in Aswân. One or two military convoys operate daily between Luxor and Aswân, (a visit to Al-Ka'b is not included in this schedule).

ASWÂN (☎ 097)

Tourist Office, at the train station, tel. 312811.
Amun Island, Club Mediterranée, Amun Island, tel. 313800, fax 317190. **Aswan Oberoi**, Elephantine Island, tel. 314666, fax 323485. **Basma Swiss Inn**, Sh. Al-Fanâdîg, tel. 310901, fax 310907. **Isis Island Hotel**, Isis Island, tel. 317400, fax 317405. **Sofitel New Cataract & Old Cataract**, Sh. Abtâl at-Tahrîr, tel. 316000, fax 316011. **Amun Tourist Village**, Sahara City (beyond the dam), tel. 480439 and 480440. **El Amir**, Corniche an-Nîlm tel. 314732. **Kalabsha**, Sh. Abtâl at-Tahrîr, tel. 322999, fax 325974. **Old Isis**, Corniche an-Nîl, tel. 315100, fax 315500. **Abu Shelib**, Sh. 'Abbâs Farîd (Basarstraße), tel. 323051. **Cleopatra**, Sh. Sa'd Zaghlûl, tel. 324001, fax 324002. **Hathur**, Corniche an-Nîl, tel. 314580. **Happi**, Sh. Abtâl at-Tahrîr, tel. 314115. **Mena**, Atlas Area, tel. 304388. **Philae**, Corniche an-Nîl, tel. 312089. **Ramses**, Sh. Abtâl at-Tahrîr, tel. 324000. *YOUTH HOSTELS:* **Youth Hostel**, Sh. Abtâl at-Tahrîr, tel. 322313.
Good oriental and international cuisine is served in the restaurants of the luxury hotels, above all in the buffet in the restaurant of the **New Cataract** hotel. An atmospheric *Candlelight Dinner*, accompanied by classical music, is available in the dining room of the **Old Cataract Hotel** – which will be familiar with fans of Agatha Christie's famous film *Murder on the Nile*! All along the Nile promenade there are rows of smaller restaurants of a high quality. Generously-portioned and well-prepared home cooking is served at the **Hotel Abu Shelib**.
Belly-dancing and Nubian folklore can be experienced in the **nightclub** of the **Aswan Oberoi hotel** and in the beautiful dining room of the **Old Cataract**. There is a **discotheque** in the **Ramses Hotel**. The **Culture Palace** (Egyptian: *Qasr as-saqâfa*) is a lot less tourist-oriented, perhaps for those travelers seeking a more authentic, less international flavor for their evening out. In this low concrete building (at the tourist market) during the winter months, Nubian folkoric events, which are well worth a visit, take place daily from 9:30-11 pm (except Fridays).
Elephantine Museum, Elephantine Island, open daily 8:30 am-6 pm, and in winter from 8 am-5 pm. **Nubian Museum**, situated opposite the Old Cataract

Hotel, 9 am-1 pm, 5-9 pm (in summer from 6-10 pm).
GETTING THERE: Flights with *Egypt Air* commute several times daily from Cairo/Luxor to Aswân. **Bus**: The *Upper Egypt Bus Company* operates runs to all the larger towns of the Nile valley, and from the Red Sea as far as Aswân. **Train**: There are several day and night trains which service the Cairo – Aswân route, but be aware that some of these routes still remain prohibited to foreign travelers due to safety and security reasons.
FERRIES: Ferries to Elephantine Island dock directly opposite the Egypt Air Office (Sh. Abtâl at-Tahrîr); the docking quay for boats traveling to the rock tombs and to Gharb Aswân lies approximately level with the tourist market.
SIGHTS: **Aswân by night** – at the *Temple of Philae* there are daily sound and light shows, available in different languages, commencing at 6 pm (6:30 pm in summertime) and 7:30 pm (summer 8 pm). The trip can be booked as a package deal at the travel office, and it includes all taxi and bus rides, boat transfers, and admission tickets.

EDFU (☎ 097)

Dar al-Salam, beside the Temple of Edfu. **El-Medina**, at the bus station. Both very basic.

NUBIAN TEMPLES

Half-day trips to **Philae** and **Kalâbsha** can be conveniently combined with a visit to the dam. As there is no public transportation here, you'll have to hire a taxi or book a tour at a travel office in Aswân. There you'll get all the information necessary about cruises between Aswân and Abû Simbel via **New Sabû'a** and **New 'Amada**.
Between Aswân and **Abû Simbel** shuttle flights operate several times daily, with a limited maximum stopover time of two hours. It is possible to combine the shuttle with a flight to/from Cairo or Luxor. The road journey by bus or taxi is now once again an option – for a long time the route was closed. But you should enquire in advance as to the safety and security in these areas.

ABÛ SIMBEL (☎ 097)

Nefertari, tel. 316402, fax 316404. **Nobaleh Ramses**, tel. 311660.
DAY TRIPS: Since April 2000 a **sound and light show** takes place every evening, which illustrates the history of the temples, in eight languages, with the help of impressive three-dimensional projections. In Abû Simbel the travel agents organize trips to see the show, and it is best to plan an overnight stay.

Southern Egypt

THE RED SEA – CORAL REEFS AND BIZARRE MOUNTAINSCAPES

THE RED SEA COAST
SINAI PENINSULA

THE RED SEA COAST

Sandy beaches as far as the eye can see, warm, crystal-clear water, 365 days of sunshine per year and a fairytale underwater world with coral reefs which are considered to be the most beautiful in the world: these are the advantages of the continental coast of the **Red Sea**, which, at most, have to be shared with the beaches of the southern Sinai Peninsula. Whether diving, snorkeling, or sailing, the range of water sports and leisure activities fulfils every wish. Furthermore, the region is comfortably located for trips to the desert or to nearby Luxor.

The tourist center for bathing and diving on the Red Sea is Hurghada, 400 kilometers south of Suez. Approximetely 25 kilometers north of Hurghada a new center has grown up in the last few years with enchanting oriental architecture and beautifully located on an artificial lagoon: ****El Gouna ❶**. Apart from numerous private houses of wealthy Egyptians, there are several hotels, ranging from good to excellent, many shops, and attractive cafés, bars and restaurants.

Those who visited **** Hurghada ❷**, which is correctly called *Al-Ghardaqa,* in

Left: In the southern Sinai, diving fun and mountain excursions can be combined.

the 1990's and who now return will scarcely recognise it. Hotels, restaurants, souvenir shops and supermarkets have shot up and have completely transformed the town center of **Dahar** and the southern harbor district of **Sigala**. It has become a mecca of tourism, with all the advantages and disadvantages. The attraction of Hurghada is that it has 32 offshore islets, the corals of which can easily be admired from glass-bottomed boats by non-divers and non-snorkelers. The **Touristic Center** of Hurghada, as it is called, begins at the round tower of the **Sheraton Hotel**, and continues southwards for many kilometers with numerous hotel complexes, many of which are very tastefully designed. Every year new complexes are added, so that public beaches outside of the holiday villages have become scarce. Isolated coves, however attractive they may be, should be avoided, as there is still a danger from mines along the whole coast. (Fenced-off areas and warning signs should be heeded at all times!)

The section of coastline at Port Safâga is especially popular with surfers. Fifteen kilometers north of Port Safâga, ****Soma Bay ❸** has developed into an elegant resort, enticing visitors with its white sandy beaches, a coral reef directly offshore and an 18-hole golf course. ***Port Safâga ❹**

Red Sea Coast and Sinai

(Arabic: *Bûr Safâja*), itself makes an interesting alternative to Hurghada. At the northern edge of the harbor town there is a series of well-maintained hotel complexes, with clean beaches and beautiful coral reefs.

The coastline south of Safâga was for a long time a well-kept secret among divers, but now it is being awakened out of its enchanted slumber. The pretty little town of *Qusair ❺, in ancient times an important harbor with the name *Leukos Limen*, has an attractive old town center with fortress ruins dating from the 16th century. But this is not what attracts the tourists, rather it is the rows of four and five-star hotels along the beaches north of the town. It is hoped that tourists will come here in their multitudes, for along the 140 kilometer stretch of coastline between Qusair and *Marsa 'Alam ❻ with its many entrancing views of the sea, numerous new resorts are being built. Marsa

Above: The Red Sea reefs belong to the most beautiful diving areas on the globe.

'Alam is still a remote village, but presumably not for very much longer. The untouched beaches and diving grounds south of the town are now being prepared for tourism; already they are easy to reach along the well-paved road that leads to the Sudan. So that the 20,000 planned hotel rooms don't remain empty long, a large new airport should be ready to start operating, in stages, from the year 2001 onwards.

THE **SINAI

The **Sinai Peninsula**, about 60,000 square kilometers in area, is not only one of the most famous but also one of the most fascinating deserts in the world.

Although the Mediterranean coast has beautiful dune landscapes and white, palm-fringed beaches, most tourists are drawn to the fascinating mountainscapes and underwater wonders of the coral reefs of Southern Sinai. But all of these features are uniquely combined on the **Gulf of 'Aqaba**. Like Hurghada, the Southern Sinai region has in the last number of years experienced an unbelievable boom, and along the 180-kilometer-long Gulf Coast, innumerable hotel complexes and diving stations have mushroomed around the superb bathing bays and quiet oases. It was soon clear, however, that this development must remain environment-friendly and so there are relatively few cases of irresponsible construction. The conservation of the coral reefs has had priority in the interests of nature, but also in the interests of the region itself.

The unrivalled center of the Sinai tourism industry is the small town of **Sharm ash-Sheikh ❼ in the south of the peninsula, where the international airport is also located. Although Egypt's diving grounds earn superlatives anyway, the coral reefs of ** Ra's Muhammad ❽ in a national park known by the same name, are considered to be the most beautiful and the richest in the world. Of the

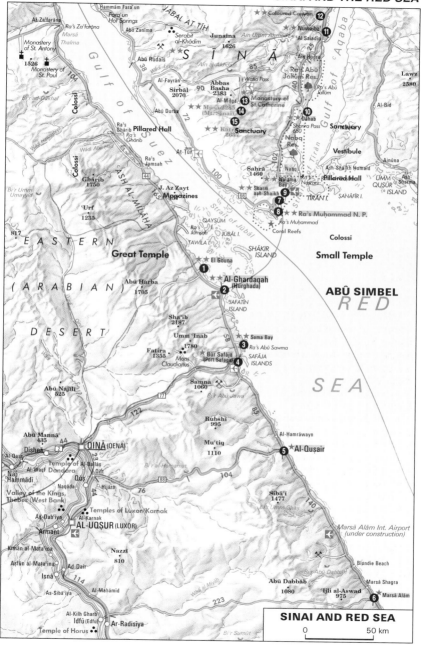

Az-Za'farāna
Ra's Za'farāna
Marsā Thalma
Monastery of St. Antony
1526
Monastery of St. Paul

JABAL AT TĪH
Hammām Fara'un Hot Springs
Fara'un Hot Springs
Abū Zanima
Serābit al-Khādim
★ Coloured Canyon ⑫
★ 'Ain Umm Aḥmad
'Al Saiadin ⑪
Junaina **1626**

S I N Ā
Abū Rudais
Al-Fayrān
'Ain al-Akhdar
85
Wādī Pass
Ra's Abū Jālūm Res.

Colossi
Bi'r ad-Dakhal

Ra's Ghārib **Pillared Hall**
Ra's Ghārib
Wadi Abū Had
Ra's Jamsah

Sirbāl **2070**
Abū Durba

Abbas Basha **2383**
Al-Milga ⑬
★★ Mūsā **2285** (M. Sinai) ⑮
★ Monastery of St. Catherine ⑭

Al-Bid
Nuwaiba'
Abū Hudra
Lawz **2580**

Dahab ⑩
Shariva Pass **680** Sanctuary

Ghārib **1750**
'Urf **1235**
44
J. Az Zayt **Magazines**

AT-Ṭūr
★★ Katu **2601** ★★ **Sanctuary**

Naqb Res.
Naqb

Vestibule
Ainūna

817

E A S T E R N

(A R A B I A N)

Sahra **1460**
Na'ama Bay
Ash-Shaikh Humad
Pillared Hall
UMM QUŞUR
Ash-Sharma
ISLAND

★ Sharm ash-Shaikh ⑦
TĪRĀN I. ŞANĀFĪR I.
⑧ ★★ Ra's Muḥammad N. P. ⑨

Great Temple

Ra's Jamsah
JUBĀL I.
QAYŞŪM I.
TĀWILA I.
SHĀKIR ISLAND
Ra's Muḥammad
Coral Reefs

Colossi

Small Temple

D E S E R T

① ★ El Gouna

Abū Harba **1705**

② ★ Al-Ghardaqah (Hurghada)
SAFĀTĪN ISLAND

ABŪ SIMBEL

Sha'ib **2187**
Umm 'Inab

Fatira **1355**
Mons Claudianus
Būr Safāja (Port Safaga)
③ ★★ Soma Bay
Ra's Abū Sawma
④ SAFĀJA ISLANDS

R E D

Abū Najili **525**

Samna **1060**
Bi'r Abū Jawa

Rubshi **995**

S E A

Abū Mannā' **435**
Dishnā
44
QINĀ (QENA)
2
Al-Qaṣr
Naj' Hammādī
Al-Waqf Qifṭ
Dandara
Temple of Al-Ballāṣ
Naqāda
Qūṣ
Hijāza
76
88

Mu'tiq **1110**
Al-Hamrāwayn
⑤ ★ Al-Quṣair
104

Valley of the Kings, Thebes (West Bank)
Ad-Dab'iya
Temples of Luxor/Karnak
Al-Karnak
AL-UQŞUR (LUXOR)
Armant
Siba'i **1477**
Bi'r Umm Ghai
Marsā Alām Int. Airport (under construction)

Kiman al-Mata'ina
Aṣfūn al-Mata'ina
Ad-Dair
Nazzi **810**
Isnā
114
As-Sibā'iya
Al-Māhāmīd
223
Abū Dabbāb **1080**
Tili al-Aswad **975**
Blondie Beach
Marsā Shagra
⑥ Marsā Alām

Al-Kilh Gharb
Idfū (Edfu)
Ar-Radisiya
Temple of Horus
Bi'r Sumūt

SINAI AND RED SEA

0 ——————— 50 km

Info p. 81

Red Sea Coast and Sinai

hotel-lined bays around Sharm ash-Sheikh **Na'ama Bay** ❾, 12 kilometers to the north, boasts a wide seaside promenade lined with the tastefully desiged flat-roofed and dome-shaped buildings of various hotels. It makes its claims as the original resort here, but the other bays, which were developed later, stretching for kilometers in both directions – from **Maya Bay** and **Ra's Umm Sid** in the south to **Shark Bay** and **Ra's Nusrânî** in the north – are nestled in the same magnificent landscape and have the same marvelous coral reefs at their doorstep.

About 70 kilometers farther north is **Dahab** ❿, a palm-tree oasis with golden-yellow sandy beaches with a variety of coral reefs, situated in front of an imposing backdrop of mountains. Here the tourist managers have also made big plans, but in spite of a number of new hotel buildings, it is still tranquil in comparison with Sharm ash-Sheikh.

Nuwaiba' ⓫ has also remained hitherto relatively untouched by the big bustle. Here there are also beautiful beaches, palm trees, turquoise-blue sea and good diving territory. From the harbor you can take a ferry across to 'Aqaba in Jordan, a trip which takes only three hours.

A really rewarding trip of about one hour by car from Nuwaiba' is the **Colored Canyon** ⓬. Here, wind and water have, in the course of thousands of years, sculpted a gorge that in some places is only shoulder wide, and laid bare the layers of sandstone in the sides of the canyon. The fascinating and unique coloring of the rock in all imaginable shades of red and ocher yellow seems more to be the work of an artist than simply the result of erosion.

In all of these resorts various excursions are offered, for example: several days of camel trekking, a starlight dinner in the desert, a trip in a glass-bottomed boat or a safari to some of the more remote valleys. Tours to St. Catherine's Monastery and the Mountain of Moses, however, will always top the list:

In its unique and dramatic setting **St. Catherine's Monastery** ⓭ rises at an elevation of 1,570 meters above a narrow valley between the mountains Jabal Mûsâ and Jabal Katrînâ. Hermits had already settled here around 300 AD, where the legend of the holy thornbush originated. The Empress Helena had a church built on this site around 330, and the Emperor Justinian incorporated it into a fortified monastery citadel with granite ramparts 12 to 15 meters in height. Ever since those days the monks have remained faithful to the Byzantine church and thus also to the Greek Orthodox church. Saint Catherine, an Alexandrian martyr from the fourth century, whose mortal remains were found in a miraculous way high up on Jabal Katrînâ, was however not adopted as the patron saint of the Sinai monastery until the Middle Ages.

The **Justinian Basilica**, from the sixth century, rises in the center of the monastery. Most of its splendid interior decoration is, however, from the 17th and 18th centuries. The beautiful Byzantine mosaics (sixth century) in the apse are famous. Directly behind the chancel is the **Chapel of the Burning Bush**, which was built over the roots of the holy thorn bush.

The walk from the monastery to the summit of **Jabal Mûsâ** ⓮ (2,285 meters), which takes around three hours, offers an unforgettable panorama. An easy winding path or the 3,000 Pilgrim Steps (very high and steep) lead up it. The nightly ascent to the top has become a regular feature on tourists' schedules. When the weather is clear, you can experience a spectacular sunrise – although, these days, rarely peace and solitude.

To find these, you must climb **Jabal Katrînâ** ⓯ which lies opposite. At 2,639 meters it is the Sinai's highest mountain. The chapel at the summit commemorates the spot where the relics of St. Catherine were discovered.

RED SEA COAST

🏠 *GETTING THERE:* **Flights:** Hurghada is serviced several times weekly by *Egypt Air* and *Air Sinai*. **Bus:** From Cairo (bus station: Mîdân Ahmad Hilmî) several buses, operated by the *Upper Egypt Bus Company*, service Hurghada daily, as well as a *Travco Sharq ad-Delta Company* bus which runs the route from Saturdays to Thursdays (departure from Sinai bus station in 'Abbâsîya northwest of Cairo). From Luxor (departure behind the Temple) there are several buses daily, in a military convoy, to Hurghada via Port Safâga. **Group taxis**: departing from Cairo to the Red Sea from Mîdân Ramsîs (main train station) and from Mîdân Gîza, in Luxor in Shâri' Abû Gûd (behind the Museum of Luxor). At the present time, out of safety reasons, these journey are only available as part of a convoy.

EL-GOUNA (☎ 065)
🛏 😊😊😊 **Mövenpick Jolie Ville** tel. 544501, fax 544505. **Paradiso Beach**, tel. 547934, fax 547933. 😊😊 **Three Corners Rihana Resort**, tel. 580025, fax 580030.

HURGHADA (☎ 065)
ℹ️ **Tourist information**, Sh. al-Mahafza, tel. 446513. 🛏 😊😊😊 **Grand Resort**, tel. 447646, fax 447649. **Hilton Resort**, tel. 442116, fax 442113. **Mariott Beach Resort**, tel. 446950, fax 446970. **Royal Azur**, Makadi Bay, 30 km south of Hurghada, tel. 5903006, fax 590304. **Sonesta Beach Resort**, tel: 443664, fax 441665. 😊😊 **Giftun Tourist Village**, tel. 442665, fax 442666. **Jasmine Holiday Village**, tel. 446442, fax 446441. 😊 **Moon Valley**, Sigala, tel. 444088. **New Ramoza**, Sigala, tel. 445065.

MARSA 'ALAM (☎ 0195)
🛏 😊😊😊 **Kahrama Beach Resort**, 27 km north of Marsa 'Alam, tel. 100261, fax 100259. **Shams Alam Beach Resort,** 45 km south, tel. only available via satellite: 00871/76/2079490, fax. 2079491.

PORT SAFÂGA (☎ 065)
🛏 😊😊😊 **Holiday Inn**, tel. 452826. **Menaville Resort**, tel. 4541761, fax 451764. **Sheraton Soma Bay Resort,** Soma Bay, tel. 545845, fax 545885. 😊😊 **Shams Safaga**, tel. 451783, fax 451780. 😊 **Sun Beach**, tel. 252658.

QUSAIR (☎ 065)
🛏 😊😊😊 **Flamenco Beach Resort**, tel. 333801, fax 333813. **Mövenpick Sirena Beach**, tel. 332100, fax 332128. **Utopia Beach Club**, 20 km south of Qusair, tel. 333227, fax 334334. 😊😊 **Fanadir**, tel. 331114.

SINAI

🏠 *GETTING THERE:* **Flights**: *Egypt Air* flies from Cairo to Al-'Arîsh, At-Tûr, Sharm ash-Sheikh and to St. Catherine's Monastery. Seasonal flights from Hurghada to St. Catherine's Monastery are also available. The international airport at Sharm ash-Sheikh belongs to the route network of numerous international charter airlines. **Bus**: The buses operated by the *East Delta Bus Company* run several times a day to Tâbâ, Nuwaiba', Dahab and Sharm ash-Sheikh, once daily there is a bus to St. Catherine's Monastery. Departure in Cairo: Sinai bus station in the 'Abbâsîya quarter. You can also travel directly by bus from Luxor to Dahab. **Speedboat**: Three times weekly a speedboat shuttles between Hurghada and Sharm ash-Sheikh, and there is a daily service connecting Nuwaiba' and 'Aqaba.

SHARM ASH-SHEIKH (☎ 062)
ℹ️ **Tourist information**, tel. 762704. 🛏 😊😊😊 **Hilton Fairouz Village**, Na'ama Bay, tel. 600136, fax 601040. **Helnan Marina Sharm**, Na'ama Bay, tel. 600751, fax 600712. **Mövenpick Victoria**, Na'ama Bay, tel. 600100, fax 600111. **Marriott Beach Resort**, Na'ama Bay, tel. 600190, fax 600188. **Seti Sharm Beach Resort**, Maya Bay, tel. 660870, fax 660147. **Sonesta Beach Resort**, Na'ama Bay, tel. 600725. 😊😊 **Clifftop Bungalow**, Sharm ash-Sheikh, tel. 600251. **Sanafir**, Na'ama Bay, tel. 600197, fax 600196. **Tiran Village**, tel. 600221. 😊 **Nubian Village**, Ras Nusrânî, tel. 314 8157. **Tropicana**, Sharm ash-Sheikh, tel. 663375.

DAHAB (☎ 062)
🛏 😊😊😊 **Novotel Dahab Holiday Village**, tel. 640304, fax 640305. **Helnan Beach Dahab Hotel**, Tourist Center, tel. 640425, fax 640428. **Swiss Inn Golden Beach**, tel. 640471, fax 640470. 😊😊 **Ganet Sinai Village**, tel. 640440. **Nubia Village**, tel. 640147. 😊 **Nesima**, tel. 640320. **New Sphinx**, tel. 640 032.

NUWAIBA' (☎ 062)
🛏 😊😊😊 **Coral Hilton Resort**, tel. 520320, fax 520027. **Tropicana**, tel. 500056, fax 500022. 😊😊 **Helnan Holiday Village**, tel. 500401. **Safari Beach Resort**, 18 km north of Nuwaiba', tel. 500445, fax 500450. 😊 **Basata Camp**, Ra's Burka, tel. 500481. **El Waha Village**, tel. 500420. **Sallyland**, 26 km north of Nuwaiba', tel. 530380.

ST. CATHERINE'S MONASTERY
🛏 😊😊😊 **Catherine Plaza**, tel. 470228. **St. Catherine Tourist Village**, Wâdî ar-Râha, tel. 470324. 😊😊 **El-Wadi el-Muqudus**, tel. 470225.
🏛 The **Monastery** is open daily (except Fri, Sun and orthodox holidays) from 9:30 am-12.30 pm.

TÂBÂ (☎ 062)
🛏 😊😊😊 **Tâbâ Hilton**, Tâbâ-Beach, tel. 530140, fax 5787044. 😊😊 **Salah el-Deen**, tel. 530340, fax 530343.

EGYPT'S GREAT GODS

The Egyptian pantheon is made up of hundreds of gods and goddesses which were worshiped in the form of fetishes, animals, plants, people and half-men half-animals. Although the peoples in very early times experienced divine power in the strength and particular abilities of animals (e.g., strength for fighting, extreme speed, the ability to fly etc.), the beginning of the period around 3000 BC saw an "anthropomorphization" of their image of god. Nevertheless, the old familiar symbols were still adhered to, and so the god Horus, for example, might be portrayed not only as falcon but also as a falcon-headed man. Alongside their many gods the Egyptians also had an abstract concept of "God": the one God, without name, who was also the creator of the world.

AMEN – His name means "The Hidden One" and points to the fact that he was originally a god of the wind – invisible, but omnipresent through his influence. His blue skin and high crown of feathers symbolize the element air. Usually portrayed as a man, he could, however, also take on the form of his holy animals, the ram and the goose. In Thebes, his center of worship, this "King of the Gods" was worshiped together with his wife **Mut** and his son, the moon god **Khonsu**.

ANUBIS – "The One in the Bandages of the Mummy" is one of the most common names for the jackal-headed god who watches over the mummification of the deceased.

KHNUM – The ram-headed god is the Lord of the Sources of the Nile, which spring from the first Nile cataract – according to the Egyptians' mythical concept of the world. As a god of creation, he makes people out of clay and forms their bodies on the potter's wheel. In his center of worship on Elephantine Island he was worshiped together with the goddesses **Satet** and **Anuket**.

HATHOR – The goddess of love, dance and music, identified with Aphrodite by the Greeks. The Egyptians called her "Queen of Heaven,"and emphasized her maternal role by portraying her as a cow or with the attributes of a cow (horns, ears). In the Theban necropolis she was revered as a goddess of death and as a tree goddess who provided food and shade.

HORUS – The falcon who flies up to heaven and whose wings span the earth like the sky was called "The Distant One." The great lights in the sky, the sun and the moon, are his eyes. In the myths surrounding Osiris, Horus is the son of Isis and Osiris. After he had punished Seth, the murderer of his father, he became the personification of the idea of the "god-kings" of Egypt.

ISIS – The loving sister-wife of Osiris is the embodiment of a mother and goddess of protection. As such she is usually portrayed in human form with the horns of a cow. She also carries the hieroglyph of a throne on her head which is used to write her name. The images which show her nursing the young Horus in her lap are regarded as direct precedents of the Christian Madonna pictures. In the cult of the dead she plays the part of a mourner with her sister **Nephthys**.

NUT – The goddess of the sky and mother of Osiris is often portrayed as a woman whose body is decorated with stars or suns and floats above the earth as a great protecting and luminescent firmament. Every night she swallows the sun as it prepares to set on the western horizon, and after its long nocturnal journey through her body, it is born again from her womb in the morning.

OSIRIS – Murdered by his jealous brother Seth and then brought back to life by his wife Isis, Osiris is the symbol of hope, resurrection and eternal life. As the

Rights: The goddess Hathor. Far right: The falcon god Horus.

lord of the afterlife he is portrayed as human, but in the form of a mummy. His crown of corn, decorated with feathers, and his skin, frequently depicted in green, refer to the fact that his fate was often identified with the cycle of the harvest year and the renewed growth of the plants.

PTAH – In the course of history the Lord of Memphis and patron of artisans and artists ascended in rank to become a universal divinity. Legends tell how he created the world with "heart and tongue," the forces of understanding and of the word of creation. Ptah is always portrayed in human form, dressed in tight robes and wearing a flat cap. The triad of Memphis is formed by Ptah, together with the lioness **Sekhmet**, revered as a goddess of war and – the reverse of her bloody, wild nature – as goddess of healing, and the god of the lotus blossom, **Nefertem**.

RA – Ra is the sun itself, which shines daily in the sky and which is honored as creator and guardian of the world. He of-

ten appears fused with Horus as **Ra-Harakhti** "Ra-Horus on the Horizon", as a falcon-man with a huge sun disk on his head. The center of worship of Ra was On, the sun city of Heliopolis. In Thebes he was fused with Amen and became the "King of the Gods" **Amen-Ra**. For a while he was elevated by the religious reformer Akhnaton to the position of sole god of Egypt who went by the name of **Aton**, portrayed by the abstract shape of the disk of the sun with hands of rays.

SETH – The god with a donkey-like head is revered as "Lord of the Desert and the Storm." Having murdered his brother Osiris, he is regarded as being the symbol of evil while playing an important part in the eternal battle for cosmic order.

THOT – The god of writing and wisdom is portrayed as an ibis-headed man or in the form of his holy animals, the ibis and the baboon. As "Lord of Time" he is associated with the moon, and for this reason carries a moon crescent and disk on his head.

CULINARY DELIGHTS

Turkish or Arabic influences can be recognized in many dishes of Egyptian cuisine; they usually require many hours of preparation time and a large variety of ingredients. But even the simplest dishes may be turned into culinary delights by adding fresh herbs and exotic spices. The most popular seasonings are coriander, cumin, chili, pepper, turmeric, cloves, ginger and sesame. Of the herbs, dill, parsley and mint are the most widely used.

Most everyday dishes do not contain meat, but this does not mean they are lacking in flavor. *Fûl* form the basis of standard home cooking. This is made of thick brown beans which can be bought for a few piasters as *fûl mudammas* – a bean stew – in the small eating houses where voluminous tin pots simmer away from early to late over a low flame. Enriched with oil, garlic, limes and a hard-boiled egg, they are generally eaten along with a round pita bread – *'aish baladî*.

Another of the thousand and one tasty *fûl* variations is *ta'mîya* (also called *filafil*) – spiced balls made from bean purée and herbs. Stuffed into an open round pita bread with onions and tomatoes, they make a hearty snack. *Kûsharî* is a speciality of the colorful mobile kitchens. It is a dish made from rice, macaroni and lentils with tomato sauce and fried onions.

On special occasions, holidays, and for guests, Egyptians will put on a lavish spread and make you feel you are indeed eating from the fleshpots of Egypt. As with Italian food, the various delicacies can be divided up into entrée, first course, main course and dessert, but with the noticeable difference that in Egypt the individual dishes are served more or less at the same time.

In Egypt the **entrée** comes in the form of delicious savories known as *mâzza*, and salads, *salatât*, which usually have little in common with salads as they are known in the West. The main exceptions are *salata baladî* (a mixed salad of finely-diced tomatoes, cucumbers, parsley and onions) and *salata tomâtim* (tomato slices with a fiery herb and garlic sauce). Other "salads" are *bâtingân* (marinated fried eggplant), *bâbâ ghanûg* (sesame paste with grilled eggplant pieces), *bîsâra* (bean purée with garlic and fried onions), *hummus* (sesame and chick pea sauce), *tahîna* (sesame paste with cumin and garlic) and *turshî* (mixed pickled made of cucumbers, carrots and turnips). These are eaten with fresh round pita bread which you dunk into the sauces.

The **first course** could be soup, or else a rice or vegetable dish, as with the following examples: *shurbat 'ads* (finely-puréed lentil soup with cumin and lime flavoring), *mulûkhîya* (a slightly bitter oily soup made from the spinach-like edible jute), *mahshî* (vegetables – zucchini, tomatoes, peppers, eggplant, white cabbage and so on, depending on the season – filled with rice and herbs), *waraq 'ainab* (vine leaves, stuffed with rice and sometimes also minced meat, and eaten warm), *bâmîya* (okra pods in tomato sauce), *mussâqa* (a casserole of eggplant and minced meat in tomato and béchamel sauce).

For the **main course** there is meat, fowl or fish, including such delicacies as *shîsh kabâb* (skewered pieces of mutton, liver and onions grilled over a charcoal fire or sometimes also prepared with chicken – then known as *firâkh*), *kabâb halla* (mutton goulash with cumin), *kufta* (small grilled balls of minced meat), *fatta* (mutton served on round flatbread in a spicy broth), *hamâm mahshî* (stuffed pigeon) and *shâwirma* (mutton grilled in thin layers on a revolving spit).

Especially in Alexandria and at the Red Sea coast you will find many good sea-

Right: Would you care for some basbûsa?

food restaurants where all sorts of fish (*samak*) and seafood, such as prawns (*gambarî*), are prepared in varied and exquisite ways.

Egyptian **desserts** are sweet and substantial, and anyone with a sweet tooth will have great trouble resisting them. A few after-dinner favorites are *baqlâwa* (a strudel made with nuts, almonds and honey), *basbûsa* (a sugar cake), *kunâfa* (a pie of wafer-thin, crisply baked pastry strips with honey and nuts), *umm 'âlî* (a hot delicacy of puff pastry, raisins, nuts, cinnamon and vanilla baked with milk and cream).

A good meal should be rounded off with a cup of *ahwa* (coffee). This is Turkish mocha which can be drunk either *mazbût* (medium sweet), *ziyâda* (very sweet) or *sâda* (without sugar). In good restaurants it is often improved by adding some cardamom and a pinch of nutmeg, following Bedouin tradition. A glass of hot *shay* (tea), perhaps with a fresh leaf of peppermint, *bi-na'na'*, also tastes wonderful.

Muslim Egyptians drink water with their meal, but in most of the restaurants (but not all!) which are used by foreigners alcoholic drinks are served. The local *Stella* is a good light beer, and the state wineries in the Delta produce light, sweet wines: *Omar Khayyam* (a strong, dry red wine), *Château Gianaclis* (a velvety, dry red wine), *Rubis d'Égypte* (a refreshing dry rosé which can, however, turn to a kind of sherry if it is stored incorrectly), *Cru de Ptolemées* (a delightful medium dry white wine), *Village Gianaclis* (a dry white wine).

There are delicious non-alcoholic drinks, such as freshly-pressed fruit juices (orange, lemon, guava and mango, according to the time of year). These are also available in a very good quality in cans. There is also *karkade* (a fruity sweet mallow tea which can be drunk hot or cold), *tamarhindî* (the sweetened juice of the tamarind).

In the Orient you do not wish the others at the table a pleasant meal: *bon appetit – hanî' an!* until after the meal!

METRIC CONVERSION

Metric Unit	US Equivalent
Meter (m)	39.37 in.
Kilometer (km)	0.6241 mi.
Square Meter (sq m)	10.76 sq. ft.
Hectare (ha)	2.471 acres
Square Kilometer (sq km)	0.386 sq. mi.
Kilogram (kg)	2.2 lbs.
Liter (l)	1.05 qt.

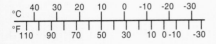

PREPARATIONS

Climate / Travel Season

Egypt is situated between the northern degrees of latitude 22° and 32° in North Africa's subtropical dry belt. As a result, a dry desert climate with mild winters and hot summers is typical. Temperature fluctuations between day and night can be as much as 17°C.

Spring is the time of the *khamsîn,* a hot dry desert wind which usually blows for many hours, and sometimes even days.

October to April is the best time to travel to Cairo and Upper Egypt. From November to April you can expect more frequent rain and cool days in Alexandria and the Delta. The same appplies to Sinai and the Red Sea, though the water of the Red Sea is never cooler than 21°C.

Clothing

It is advisable to take light cotton clothes, comfortable shoes and some form of head covering. You should also pack some warm things for the winter months, as it can sometimes get quite chilly, even during the day. Neither too informal nor too scanty clothing is suitable – even when the barometer climbs to unaccustomed heights. But Egyptians have now, unfortunately, had to get used to the fact that Western visitors would rather undress than dress in the summer heat. In a time of a resurgence of traditional values, this can be offensive to Egyptians – bare arms and legs are unseemly for both women and men in Egypt. Sleeveless shirts, shorts and tight-fitting trousers should be avoided – not only in mosques and churches.

Entry Requirements / Visas

To enter the country you need a passport which is valid for at least a further six months and an Egyptian visa. You can obtain a one-month visa on arrival at any Egyptian airport or harbor with the exception of Sharm ash-Sheikh. Even if you have a South African visa in your passport, you can once again travel to Egypt. No visas are issued at border stations on land routes (except Eilat/Tâbâ). A visa with three months validity can be obtained from Egyptian consulates. Forms may be obtained by sending a stamped and self-addressed envelope to your nearest Egyptian consulate (see p. 92/93).

Customs and Import Regulations

All travelers recieve a customs declaration form on arrival, which recently have only been infrequently inspected. However, for your own good you should fill it out and have it stamped (!), in the event that you'll be taking more than US $500 in currency or checks with you when you leave the country. Video cameras must be declared and entered in your passport. Egyptian currency taken into or out of the country may not exceed LE 20. Importation of the following items are tax free up to the amount given: 200 cigarettes or 25 cigars or 200 grams of tobacco; one liter of spirits; items intended for person use. Toll-free goods can be bought at Cairo International Airport even after arrival in the country.

Currency / Foreign Exchange

The Egyptian Pound (abbreviated LE for *Livre Égyptienne*) is the country's unit of currency. It is divided up into 100 *pias-*

ters – abbreviated PT. In Egyptian Arabic the pound is called the *Ginéh* and the piaster *Qirsh* (pronounced "irsh" in Cairo).

1 LE cost approx. 0,3 US$ in September 2000. The following rates can be used for orientation purposes:

1 US $ . . . . 3.6653 LE
1 Pound Sterling . . . . . . 5.3081 LE

The usual credit cards and travelers' checks are accepted just about everywhere in tourist and urban centers, unlike Eurocheques, which are only accepted in a few banks and at the airport. Bank branches in hotels, unlike regular banks, usually have a 24-hour service. You should keep your exchange receipts until you leave, as they'll be required if you wish to exchange any Egyptian pounds you may have left at the end of your visit.

Health Care

Vaccinations are not required to travel to Egypt. But people traveling from infected areas, or who have passed through an infected area in the previous six days, must have yellow fever and cholera vaccinations. Inquire at the appropriate health office before you travel.

A gamma globulin injection is recommended, as this gives a certain amount of protection against hepatitis A, lasting about six weeks. For the summer months it is advisable to take precautions against malaria. Private medical travel insurance is strongly recommended.

A medical kit for the journey should contain medicine against all kinds of colds (the most common illness which you will catch in Egypt!), fever, flu, digestive and circulatory problems. A disinfectant salve for wounds, adhesive bandages and dressings are just as important as a sun cream with a high blocking factor, and insect sprays or lotions.

The most common cause of those unpleasant, but mostly harmless, digestive tract disorders is drinking beverages which are too cold. The great difference in temperature between day and night,

and excessively air-conditioned hotel rooms and buses can often bring on colds. Because of the danger of contracting bilharziasis, you should only swim in chlorinated water or the sea; never in the Nile, fresh-water lakes or canals.

ROUTES TO EGYPT
By Air

Cairo International Airport is the hub of international air traffic between Europe, Africa and Asia. It is serviced by most international airlines. The state-owned Egyptian carrier *Egypt Air* runs regular flights from New York, Los Angeles, Copenhagen, Helsinki, Stockholm, Bangkok, Bombay and Manila, among other cities. There are also regular flights from all major European cities. A number of charter airlines offer year-round bargain tickets and package arrangements. The direct flights to Hurghada, Luxor, Sharm ash-Sheikh- or Aswân are very attractively priced.

TRAVEL WITHIN EGYPT
A Few Words About Security

Terrorist attacks carried out in recent years against tourists have created great anxiety for those traveling to Egypt. Although the situation has calmed down since the massacre in Luxor on November 17, 1997, official agencies still emphasize a certain security risk in Central Egypt. Although militant Islamic groups have explicitly declared that they will no longer attack foreigners and, since 1997, there has been no further attack on tourists – it cannot be ruled out that in Islamic centers, such as Minyâ or Asyût, there is a risk of being caught in conflicts between Islamic groups and state authorities. For current information contact the Foreign Affairs Office of your country.

While there are no restrictions per se on tourists, certain routes and places, and less frequently even larger regions, may be subject to temporary closure to tourists, showing that the Egyptian govern-

Guidelines

ment is very concerned about the safety of visitors to the country. Therefore, certain tourist trains to the south have military escorts. In the Nile Valley between Minyâ and Luxor, between Luxor and Aswân or Dandara and Abû Simbel, private vehicles, taxis transporting tourists and tourist buses may travel only with a police escort. If you're traveling with an organized tour, your tour operator will take care of all organizational problems. If you are traveling on your own, find out well in advance what the current safety regulations for specific regions are. Information can be obtained through travel agents, tourist offices and hotel staff.

By Rail

Rail is a good and very cheap means of transportation in the Delta and Nile Valley. There are two daytime and several night trains of the Egyptian State Railroad with sleeping cars which travel the Cairo-Luxor-Aswân route. In addition, there are two international *Wagon Lits* trains per night. Journey time is about 11 hours to Luxor and 15 hours to Aswân. Tickets should be purchased at least a week before departure from a travel agency or train station.

Trains shuttle almost hourly between Cairo and Alexandria and several times a day there is an express train (journey time 2.5 hours). In summer there is a night train with sleeping cars from Cairo or Alexandria to Matrûh, for which tickets and seats should be reserved at least one day before departure at the appropriate station. Reservations are especially necessary during the peak season!

By Air

Internal flights in Egypt are no longer as cheap as they were, but apart from problems with sandstorms in spring they are usually punctual and reliable.

Egypt Air flies the routes Cairo-Alexandria, Cairo-Luxor, Cairo-Aswân-Abû Simbel, Cairo-Hurghada, Cairo-

Sharm ash-Sheikh several times a day, as well as the Cairo-Dhâkla-Khârga, Cairo-Matrûh, Luxor-Hurghada, Luxor-Sharm ash-Sheikh, Aswân-Sharm ash-Sheikh routes several times a week. Egypt Air offices in Cairo: Nile Hilton, tel. 759-703, Sheraton Gîza, tel. 3488630, 9 Sh. Tal'at Harb, tel. 3930381.

Air Sinai regularly shuttles between Cairo, Luxor, Hurghada and the Sinai. Main airports in the Sinai are Sharm ash-Shaîkh, At-Tûr, St. Catherine's Monastery and Al-'Arîsh and since quite recently Ra's an-Naqb near Tâbâ. There is an airline office in the arcade of the Nile Hilton Hotel at Mîdân at-Tahrîr, Cairo, tel. 760948. All Air Sinai flights must be booked there, even if you are flying to the Sinai from Hurghada or Luxor.

By Ship

A Nile cruise has always been considered the classical Egyptian journey. Of the 400 luxury hotel ships that ply the river, the majority travel the standard route between Dandara and Aswân. In addition, a few ships offer three to four-day cruises on the lake of the Aswân dam to the temples of New 'Amâda and New Sabû'a, as well as Abû Simbel, still accessible only by water. Cruises are usually sold as part of a package, including full board and guided tours of regional sights. Bookings can be made at almost any travel agency or most major hotels.

A trip of several days from Luxor to Aswân, or vice versa, on board a *feluka,* a large sailboat, is a unique experience. You sleep on deck in the open air, the skipper is responsible for providing blankets and full board – he shops en route and cooks for his guests. The price is agreed upon beforehand.

Car Rental and City Taxis

Car rental firms, such as Avis, Bita, Budget and Hertz, are represented in all the large hotels and at the airport. To hire a car you must be over 21 years old and have had a driver's license for over one year, plus an international driver's license. The price of rental cars is considerably lower than in Europe; credit card users usually do not have to pay a deposit.

If you do not want to drive, you can get a car and driver at a reasonable price at most travel agents or the state hire company *Misr Limousine*, tel. 2599813. Taxi drivers often offer to take people on tours of the sights and surroundings. The fare should be agreed upon in advance.

Tours

Organized tours – from day excursions to trips lasting several days, with or without a guide – can be booked at all of the larger Egyptian travel agencies. The state travel agent *Misr Travel*, with branches in all of the interesting tourist towns, has a fixed timetable of daily tours and visits.

PRACTICAL TIPS

Accommodation

The official classification system of Egyptian hotels, from 1 to 5 stars, does not correspond to the Western sytem. The border between the middle category and luxury class is unclear and hotels often seem to be over or underrated.

🟢🟢🟢 Prices in the upper categories (4 and 5-star) lie between US$ 65 and 200 for a double room.

🟢🟢 In the middle category (3-star) you must reckon with US $ 50 to 80 and there are large regional differences.

🟢 In more basic hotels (2-star to clean guest house) you can expect to pay a 75 – 150 Egyptian pounds (approx. US $ 50) for a double room. In addition to the price for the room, 10 percent service charge and 12 percent tax are generally added.

Alcohol

Islam is the state religion and alcohol is therefore restricted. International hotels, restaurants and a few licensed businesses offer Egyptian wine and local beer.

Baksheesh

Service tips of 10 to 15 perent are usually expected in hotels (no matter how basic the establishment) and restaurants. In addition, a little baksheesh is expected for every small service. This is not only true of hotel staff, taxi-drivers, boat owners, carriage and camel drivers, but also of attendants at mosques, temples and tombs, who usually try to "earn" their baksheesh by pointing out particularly beautiful camera shots. Amounts equivalent to US $0.50 to $1.50 are usually suitable, and it is advisable to keep enough spare change ready. Ballpoint pens and lighters are treasured items, which no traveler should be without! Children who beg should not be given any money.

Baksheesh is a social obligation which must be met by those who can afford it. All small services, including those outside of the tourist sector, are paid off in this way. This creates socially acceptable employment and extra income for many people for whom it is, given their low wages, of vital importance.

Banks

In international hotels in Cairo and at the airport, banks are open 24 hours. All other banks are open from 9:30 am to 12:30 pm Monday-Thursday, and on Sunday from 9:30 am to noon.

Electricity

Voltage is 220V, but you'll need an adapter for grounded plugs. In Egypt a small flashlight is an absolute necessity, be it for hotel power cuts or when visiting temples and tombs which can be badly, or not at all, lit. A voltage stabilizer is recommended for electronic appliances.

Filming and Photography

Egypt is a photographer's paradise, but a few written – and unwritten – rules should be observed: Photographing military installations, bridges or harbors is not permitted. In most ancient Egyptian

Guidelines

tombs, temples and museums, taking photographs or making videos is allowed after payment of a fee, but only without flashbulbs. You can buy tickets allowing photography at the entrance booths, except for Thebes West (see *Guidepost: Luxor / Thebes West*, p. 62/63).

If you wish to take a photograph of someone, you should always be sure to ask their permission first. One simple gesture can overcome any language barrier! A little baksheesh is also suitable, if it is requested. Slums or poverty should not be photographed, as you may insult peoples' feelings and they may also on occasion react in an extreme manner.

Food and Drink

Hygiene in large cities and tourist centers is very good. But care should be taken with green salads, unpeeled fruit and raw vegetables, mayonnaise and ice-cream. Tap water is on the whole clean, but so strongly chlorinated that you will simply not want to drink it for that precise reason. Mineral water is safer.

Holidays

January 1, February 22 (Day of Unity), April 25 (Return of the Sinai), May 1 (International. Workers' Day), June 18 (Withdrawal of British Troops), July 23, (Anniversary of the Revolution), October 6 (Invasion of the Sinai), October 24 (Suez Day), Dec. 23 (Victory Day).

Information

A wealth of useful information journey preparation, as well as for learning more about the country, is now available on the internet. The official website of the Egyptian Ministry of Tourism is at: http://www.touregypt.net. Detailed hints and travel information are also available at http://www.sis.gov.eg/egyptinf. There are short texts on all Egyptian cities and much practical information such as addresses for hotels, cruise ships, car rental at http://www.tourism.egnet.net.

For up-to-date statistics and short background texts on economic themes see Middle East Business Information: http://www.ameinfo.com/facts/egyptpeo. htm. A must for all who are infected with "Egypt fever" are the culture websites. Guardians Egypt and the Egypt WWW Index are outstanding texts and source collections and have link lists to all other topics of Egyptian culture and history: http://www.ce.eng.usf.edu.pharos.

There is, of course, also the conventional method of obtaining information, from the **Egyptian Tourist Office**. *UK*: Egyptian State Tourist Office, Egyptian House, 170 Picadilly, London W1V 9DD, tel. 0044-171-4935282, 0044-171--4080295. *USA*: Egyptian Tourist Authority, 630 Fifth Avenue, suite 1706, New York, NY 10111, tel. 001-212--3322570, fax 9566439, e-mail egyptoursp@aol.com, Egyptian Tourist Authority, 8383 Wilshire Blvd. suite 215, Beverly Hills, CA 90211, tel. 001-213-6538815, fax 6838961. In Egypt you can visit the local tourist offices (addresses in the info pages under the place names at the end of each chapter.)

Opening Times

Friday is the day of rest, but that is only for offices, official organizations and banks. Most shops are open from 2 p.m. at the latest (after Friday prayers). Many business people, international companies and entrepreneurs of the Coptic faith, on the other hand, shut up shop on Sunday. Even the bazaar is dead on Sundays (not Fridays!). Being between the two, Saturday can form a weekend with either the Islamic Friday or Christian Sunday. Business hours are quite regular from Monday to Thursday: 9 am to 7 pm in the winter (until 8 pm on Thursdays), 9 am to 1:30 pm and 5 to 8 pm in the summer (until 9 pm on Mondays and Thursdays). Grocery stores may open until late in the evening.

Most mosques, temples and tombs can be visited from 7 am-4 pm in winter, and in summer from 6 am-5 pm. The large museums are usually open daily from 9 am-4 pm, the smaller ones from 9 am-1 pm. On Fridays some shut at 11:15 am for two hours during prayer time. During the month of Ramadân other opening times apply. The Egyptian Museum in Cairo closes at 3 pm, the museum in Luxor at 3:30 pm, and most excavation sites at 5 pm, but tickets are only sold until 3:30 pm So you should check beforehand.

Pharmacies

There are pharmacies with a comprehensive selection in Cairo and every large town. As international pharmaceutical concerns also produce in and for Egypt you can get the usual medications – often without a prescription. If you need a certain medicine, you should be able to name its active substances, as trade names vary.

Post

Letters and postcards are best mailed from hotels. Stamps can usually be bought at shops selling postcards. Public mailboxes are blue for foreign airmail and red for internal Egyptian mail. The main Post Office in Cairo, at Mîdân 'Ataba 15, opens daily from 8 am to 8 pm.

Prices

Favorable exchange rates make Egypt a fairly cheap country to visit on the whole. The most notable exception to this rule are the entrance prices charged at tourist attractions. You will have to pay up to about US $14 per person for tickets. This money is needed, however, for the maintenance and restoration of the monuments. By showing an International Student Identity Card students can receive discounts.

Shopping

Egypt is regarded as a true paradise for souvenir hunters – with all the positive and negative aspects. As is the custom in the Orient, you have to haggle about prices. The first rule of this game is: Take your time! Everything else is a question of intuition and your own business talent.

Classic mementos from Egypt include: copper and brass goods, such as trays with ornamental engravings or inlay work, candlesticks, lamps, pots and dishes; fine woodwork with mother-of-pearl inlays which can be bought as boxes, board games or wall plates – sometimes you'll find wonderfully intricate *mashrabîya* lattice-work of a transportable size (e.g., elegant mirror frames or folding screens); woven carpets with beautiful geometric patterns or the well-known pictorial carpets with naive depictions of nature and country life – traditionally from Harranîya and Kirdâsa (near Gîza), but now found everywhere, even in the Sinai; leather goods of all kinds made from camel and buffalo hide, such as belts, bags, shoes, cushions, etc., which are very good value (though you should check the quality of the work); gold and silver jewelry in various forms and price categories; ancient Egyptian motifs, such as scarabs, ankhs – the Egyptian symbol of life – and cartouches, into which you can have your name worked in hieroglyphics, are both original and attractive. Then there is Egyptian clothing, such as the *gallâbîya*, the traditional ankle-length gown worn by men, which can be made in one day. Especially imaginative creations have been invented mainly for tourists: cotton sweatshirts and T-shirts with hieroglyphic or other Egyptian motifs, and summer clothes and housewear in the *gallâbîya* style.

The colorful glittering belly-dancing costumes are a good idea for carnival time. Perfume essences and oils which are offered by veritable masters of ceremony in their seductively fragrant plush grottos are a pleasure not to be missed! There are spices, of which there are a great variety; papyri painted with Pharaonic motifs which vary in quality and size, and can be bought everywhere –

in many papyrus shops (especially those near to the Gîza pyramids) there are demonstrations showing how the papyri are made from the papyrus plant according to ancient Egyptian tradition. So-called "antique" items (which are guaranteed to be at least three days old) are on offer everywhere. A few licensed dealers in Cairo and Luxor do sell real antique items now and again, along with well-made replicas. Trade in, and export of, genuine antiques (items over 100 years old) is illegal.

Telecommunications

To call Egypt from abroad, dial +20 plus the area code (without the first "0") plus the number. To place a call to the U.S. or Canada from Egypt, dial country code 001; for the U.K. 0044; for Ireland 00353; for Australia 0061.

Time

Egyptian time is Greenwich Mean Time plus two hours; Eastern Standard Time plus seven hours. As Daylight Savings Time has recently been introduced in Egypt, the difference remains constant throughout the year.

EGYPT IN STATISTICS

Total Area: 1.002 million square kilometers of which 3.5 percent is settled or in agricultural use.
Population (2000): 68,5 million, of which 45 percent reside in the cities.
Average population growth: +1,9 percent.
Average life expectancy: 66 years.
Employment: 34 percent agriculture, 22 percent industry, 44 percent service sector. Unemployment rate 8 percent.
Form of government: presidential republic with a multi-party system; President: Husnî Mubârak (National Democratic party, since 1981).
Administrative form: 26 Provinces (Governorates).

ADDRESSES

Airline Offices

The main offices of all the large airlines are located in Cairo's city center around the Mîdân at-Tâhîr.
Air Canada: 26 Sh. Mohamed Bassiouni. **Air Sinai:** Nile Hilton Hotel, tel. 760948. **American Airlines:** 20 Sh. El Gehad, Mohandessin, tel. 345-5707. **British Airways:** 1 Sh. Abdel Salam Aref, tel. 762852 (airport: 671741). **Delta:** 17 Sh. Ismail Mohamed, Zamalek, tel. 342-0861. **El Al:** 5 El Maqrizi, Zamalek, tel. 340-8912, 341-1429. **Egypt Air:** Nile Hilton, Md. Tahrir, tel. 575-9703; Sheraton Gîza, tel. 348-8630, 348-9122; 9 Md. Talaat Harb, tel. 392-2835, 393-0381; Sheraton Hotel, Md. Galaa, tel. 348-8630. **TWA:** 1 Sh. Kasr El Nil, tel. 574-9904/08/10/17. **United:** 42 Sh. Abdel Khalek Tharwat, tel. 3908099/5090.

Automobile Club

Automobile et Touring Club d' Egypt (ATCE), 10 Sh. Qasr an-Nil, Cairo, tel. (2) 574-3176/3355; 15 Sh. Salah Salem, Alexandria, tel. (3) 481494/5.

Embassies and Consulates

In Egypt: *CANADA:* 6 Sh. Mohamed Fahmy El Sayed, Garden City, tel. 354-3110, fax. 3563548. *IRELAND:* 3 Sh. Abu El Feda, Zamalek, tel. 340-8264, fax. 3412863. *UK:* 7 Sh. Ahmed Ragheb, Garden City, tel. 354-0852. *USA:* 3 Sh. Lazoughli, Garden City, tel. 355-7371.
Abroad:. *CANADA:* Egyptian Embassy, 454 Laurier Ave. East, Ottowa, Ontario K1N 6R3, tel. (613) 234-4931/35/58; Egyptian consulate Montreal, 3754 Cote des Neiges, Montreal, Quebec H3H 7V6, tel. (514) 937-7781/2. *IRELAND:* Egyptian Embassy,12 Clyde Rd., Dublin 4, tel. (1) 606566/718. *UK:* Egyptian Embassy, 26 South St., London W1Y 6DD, tel. (171) 499-2401; Egyptian Consulate, 2

Lowndes St., London SW1, tel. (171) 235-9777. *USA:* Egyptian Embassy, 3521 International CTM. W., Washington, DC 20008, tel. (202) 895-5400, fax. (202) 224-4319/5131; Egyptian Consulate, 1110 2nd Ave. New York, NY 10022, tel. (212) 759-7120/1/2; Egyptian consulate, 3001 Pacific Ave., San Francisco, CA 94115, tel. (415) 346-9700/2.

Egyptian Tourism Authority (ETA) Offices

In Egypt: Misr Travel Tower, Md. Abassia, Cairo (Headquarters), tel. (2) 285-4509, 284-1970, fax. 285-4363. **Abroad:** *CANADA:* 1253 McGill College Avenue, Suite 250, **Montreal**, Quebec H3B 2Y5, tel. (514) 861-4420, fax. 861-8071. *UK:* Egyptian House, 170 Picadilly, **London** W1V 9DD, tel. (171) 493-5282, fax. 408-0295. *US:* **New York**, NY 10111, tel. (212) 336-3570, fax. 956-6439.

LANGUAGE GUIDE

Classical Arabic is the official language but is only used in radio, television and sermons. Everyday language is the Egyptian dialect of Arabic. The Arabic article is "al" (in dialect it is pronounced "el" or "il"). If the next word begins with d, n, r, s, z, or t, it is assimilated to ad, an, ar, as, az and at.

â, ê, î, ô and *û* are long vowels which are stressed.

h is an aspirate and is pronounced, even at the end of words (as the ch in German Kir**ch**e – phonetic symbol ç)

kh is pronounced like the *Scottish* lo**ch** or *Spanish* Rio**j**a (phonetic symbol x))

z is a voiced s

sh – as in English

' is an apostrophe which marks the glottal stop between two vowels.

' is a typical Arabic voiced gutteral sound which is "choked" out of the voice box always in combination with a vowel.

gh is a voiced fricative positioned at the back of the soft palate and sounds like the French r.

q is a gutteral k (not kw) which in Egypt is usually silent. One exception is e.g. Al-Qâhira (Cairo).

y correspomds to the English y in yacht.

In Arabic men (m) and women (f) are addressed differently. In conversation the familiar form of 'you' is normally used, if the conversation is formal, or you wish to be especially polite, the word *hadritak* (m) or *hadritik* (f) is added at the beginning of sentences and questions.

What is your name?	*ismak ê? (m) ismik ê?(f)*
My name is...	*ismi ...*
Where are you from?	*inta (m)/ inti (f) minên?*
I am from...	*ana min ...*
I don't understand.	*ana mish fâhim (m), ana mish fahma (f).*
How do you say that in...?	*ê ma'na da bi-l- ...?*
Arabic	*'arabi*
English	*inglîzi*
taxi	*taks*
bus	*bâs*
subway	*metro*
train	*qatr*
plane	*tayyâra*
train station	*mahatta*
airport	*matâr*
street	*shâri'* (abbr. Sh.)
square	*mîdân* (abbr. Md.)
left	*'ash-shimâl*
right	*'al-yimîn*
straight	*'ala tûl*
pyramid/pyramids	*haram/ahrâm*
temple	*ma'bad*
tomb	*maqbara*
museum	*mathaf*
church	*kinîsa*
mosque	*masgid oder gâmi'*
market	*sûq*

Guidelines

tomatoes	. . . .	*tamâtim*
cucumber	. . . .	*khiyâr*
salad	. . . .	*salata*
grapes	. . . .	*'ainab*
apples	. . . .	*tuffâh*
apricots	. . . .	*mishmish*
bananas	. . . .	*môs*
strawberries	. . . .	*faraula*
dates	. . . .	*balâh*
bread	. . . .	*'aish*
coffee	. . . .	*qahwa*
tea	. . . .	*shai*
one kilogram	. . . .	*wâhid kîlû*
one pound	. . . .	*nuss kîlû*
one hundred grams	. . . . . .	*mît grâm*
good	. . . .	*kuwayyis/tamâm*
expensive	. . . .	*ghali*
Do you have...?	. . . .	*fîh?*
No, we don't have...	. . . . .	*la, mafîsh*
How much does that cost?	. . . .	
		bi-kam da?
Thanks, that's plenty	. . . .	
		shukrân, kifâya kida.

Numbers

Although we use Arabic numerals, true Arabic numerals look quite different:

0	٠	*sifr*
1	١	*wâhid*
2	٢	*itnên*
3	٣	*talâta*
4	٤	*arba'a*
5	٥	*khamsa*
6	٦	*sitta*
7	٧	*sab'a*
8	٨	*tamanya*
9	٩	*tis'a*
10	١٠	*'ashara*
11	١١	*hidâshar*
12	١٢	*itnâshar*
13	١٣	*talatâshar*
14	١٤	*arba'tâshar*
15	١٥	*khamastâshar*
16	١٦	*sittâshar*
17	١٧	*sab'atâshar*
18	١٨	*tamantâshar*
19	١٩	*tis'atâshar*
20	٢٠	*'îshrîn*
21	٢١	*wâhid wa-'ishrîn*

30	٣٠	*talatîn*
50	٥٠	*khamsîn*
100	١٠٠	*miyya*
1,000	١٠٠٠	*alf*

AUTHOR

Eva Ambros, project editor and author of Nelles Guide Egypt, studied Egyptology, classical Arabic and the languages of Christian cultures in the Orient. Moreover, she spent twelve years working in Egypt as a guide for study tours. She currently lives in Munich, where she works as a freelance author and translator.

PHOTOGRAPHERS

Fischer, Peter	20, 34, 55
Janicke, Volkmar E.	12
Legde, Benjamin W.G.	3, 8, 9, 15, 16, 21, 23, 25, 26, 31, 39, 41, 44, 49, 51, 53, 57, 59, 61, 66, 68, 71, 72, 74, 83 l., 83 r.
Mielke, Harald	76, 78
Nelles, Günter	70
Riepl, Ingo (Silvestris)	Cover
Skupy, Jitka	29
Spring, Anselm	42, 64, 85
Thiele, Klaus	10/11.

INDEX